THE **ADLARD COLES** BOOK OF

RADAR

BÖRJE WALLIN

GW00771375

ADLARD COLES NAUTICAL
LONDON

Contents

Part 1
Getting started

1 Starting up

Radar is a fantastic instrument for navigation and collision avoidance. However, while most instruments give you hard facts, radar gives you information that needs to be interpreted. It is very different from the:

- Echosounder, which gives you the depth.
- Log, which provides speed and distance.
- Compass, which gives your course.
- GPS, which gives your position.

On the radar screen you can see blobs made by dots of light. These blobs show that the radar has detected something, but it cannot tell you what that 'something' is, and interpreting these blobs is a kind of art. Initially you have to adjust the radar so it will show you what you want to see. Then you have to interpret the picture and draw your conclusions.

This book describes the art of using radar both in confined waters and offshore. It assumes familiarity with the rules for the prevention of collisions at sea (COLREGS) and with elementary navigation. Technical descriptions are only included when necessary, as you will find more advanced technical explanations in the owner's handbook for your particular radar set.

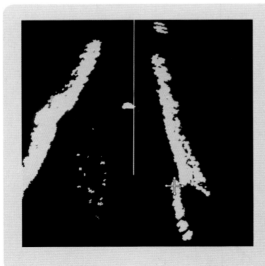

A radar image contains a lot of information, but it needs interpretation. Here, our vessel is in the centre of the radar picture, heading along the line from the centre and straight up, commonly referred to as the Heading Mark.

The parts of a radar set

Radome antenna.

Open antenna.

All radar antennae rotate when in use, but radome antennae are protected from wind and weather by stationary covers.

As the scanner (antenna) revolves, the transmitter emits very short pulses of energy, each lasting less than a microsecond, but repeated anything up to 3000 times per second, depending on the range at which the radar is operating.

Microseconds later it receives that reflected energy back as an echo from any radar-reflective targets within range.

The sensitive receiver would be irreparably damaged if it were ever subjected directly to the very powerful pulses of energy from the transmitter, so it is protected by a device called the Transmit/Receive (T/R) cell, which isolates the receiver whenever the transmitter is transmitting.

The receiver amplifies the returning echoes and then sends them to the display.

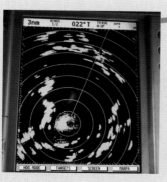

On the radar screen, returning echoes are represented by blobs called 'contacts'. The bearing and distance of a contact from the centre of the screen (which is the position of your own vessel) shows the direction and range of the detected object. The radar computes the distance by measuring the elapsed time for the pulse to return. The direction on the screen depends on the direction of the antenna when it received the returning pulse.

Modern radars on small pleasure craft are controlled by a combination of knobs, buttons and menus. Because a radar set can last 20 years or more, a navigator may find himself using a variety of sets, requiring different procedures for adjustment.

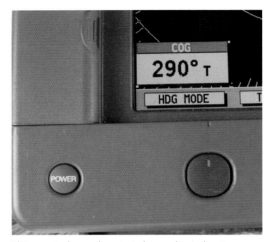

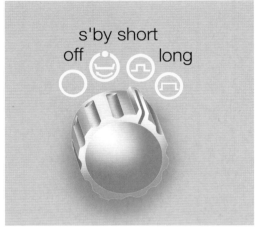

This particular radar starts by pushing the Power button.

This radar starts when the knob is set to 'Standby'.

Every radar set consists of an antenna, a display and the electronics that deal with the signals.

On older radar screens the image was drawn by the 'sweep', which is seen as a line rotating at the same speed as the antenna. This technology, in which the picture is preserved for a short while by the 'afterglow' in the fluorescent layer of a Cathode Ray Tube (CRT), results in an incomplete image on the screen.

A modern set for small craft has a flat screen that uses a Liquid Crystal Display (LCD). In this type of set the contacts are stored in a picture memory, and renewed for every antenna revolution. The entire image is seen all the time, which can make the picture easier to interpret. LCD images are also easily visible in daylight.

However, with regard to adjustment of the set and interpretation of the image, there is very little practical difference between different types of display.

No pulse-emitting radar shows a picture immediately after switching on because the set has to warm up, but when the set is ready to transmit, the message 'Standby' will appear on the screen. After that time, pushing a button labelled 'Transmit' or 'TX' will activate transmission of microwaves and the radar may or may not start to show a

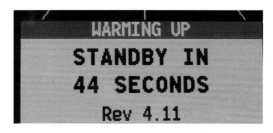

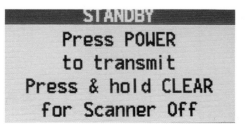

picture, depending on how the other controls are set. When in Standby, the radar is warm and ready to use but is not actually transmitting, so returning the radar to Standby will save energy if you take a break away from the set, but the radar will still be instantly useable.

Getting a picture

When the radar set is switched to 'Transmit', what you first see on the radar screen varies, depending on the settings in use when the radar was last switched off and the differences in sea and weather conditions between then and now. Because of this the image will almost certainly need adjustment and you may not even have an image at all. When you need to adjust the image from scratch, proceed as below.

Rain and sea clutter
Start by turning the Rain Clutter and Sea Clutter controls to zero. These can be adjusted later to diminish annoying contacts from rain and waves, and adjusting them at the beginning can reduce useful contacts during the initial set-up.

Rain and Sea Clutter controls on a modern radar, controlled by 'soft' buttons.

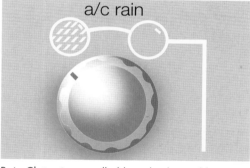

Rain Clutter is controlled by a knob on older sets.

Brilliance
Next you need to adjust Brilliance, increase it until the text and graphics are clear but not dazzling. This control adjusts the general brightness of the screen. On some radar sets it may have another name, for example Brightness or Light.

Change Brilliance as the ambient light around the radar changes. Generally, it's recommended to adjust the radar screen until it's just bright enough to be seen clearly, but not so bright that you struggle to distinguish the details.

Many sets have the facility to change the colours so they won't disturb your night vision.

Some monochrome radar displays also have a control known as Contrast which adjusts the characteristics of the display to suit the intensity and angle of the approaching light, and the direction from which it is being viewed. Adjusting it is simply a matter of trial and error to get the best picture for the prevailing conditions.

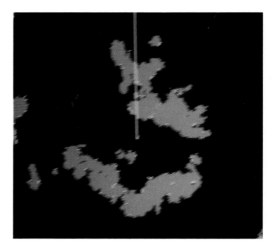

Tune

Now proceed with Tune. This function tunes the receiver to the frequency that is being transmitted. Many modern radar sets have an automatic Tune, but you may encounter sets with both automatic and manual Tune.

If Tune needs to be set manually, 'home in' on the best adjustment by turning the control to and fro. There is usually an indicator to show the optimal setting (in the picture below, this is above the Tune bar).

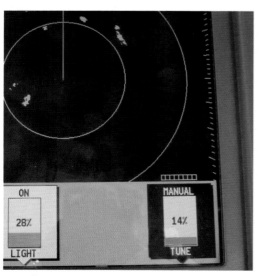

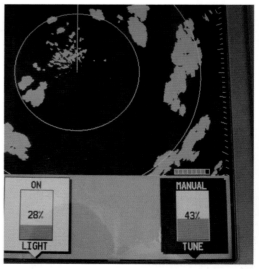

The effect of Tune control. There is too little Tune in the left picture and optimal Tune in the right picture. (Note that the Brilliance control – seen on the left in the pictures – is called Light on this radar.)

Gain

You now need to adjust the Gain control.

This makes the contacts brighter, so you should now have a picture on the screen. How you adjust the Gain control depends on what you want to see. To start with, adjust Gain to show a light background speckle, then as you encounter different situations and conditions, adjust it accordingly. In a river or another narrow passage, the Gain ought to be low to create sharp contacts of the shoreline. When land and navigational beacons are more distant, more Gain is needed to see their contacts.

If you enter a narrow channel with Gain adjusted for the open sea, the contacts from the shorelines will probably be too strong, blurring or even making the entrance invisible.

In the pictures below you can see how the picture changes when Gain is low (left) and high (right). High gain strengthens and enlarges the contacts. For example, in the right-hand picture the land contacts look more like a solid land mass than a lot of small islands. (Also, to the left of our vessel a lot of the contacts are likely to be from waves!)

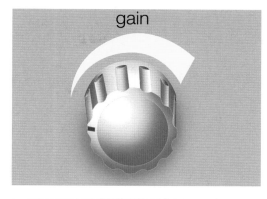

The Gain control on this radar is activated by pressing the 'soft key' below the screen and adjusted with the 'touch pad' on the right.

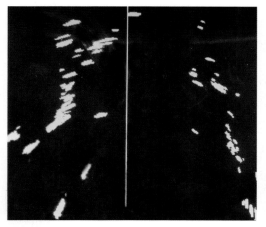

Low Gain.

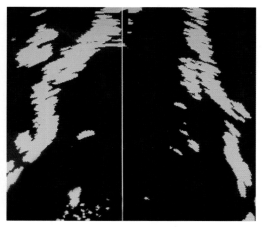

High Gain.

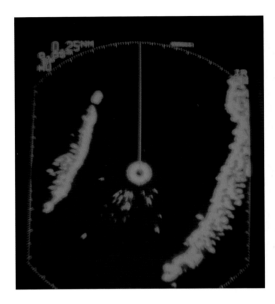
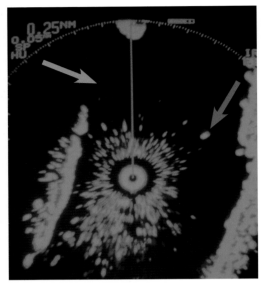

Similary, the picture on the left, above, shows a screen with low Gain. The picture to the right is the same, but with increased Gain. The extra contacts close to the vessel are mainly sea clutter, but increased Gain has revealed a spar buoy (see red arrow). There is also another spar buoy (see green arrow) but more Gain is needed to show it. Therefore, correct Gain depends on what the navigator wishes to see at any particular moment.

Range

All radars have a control to alter the Range, which is the distance shown from the centre of the picture to its outer edge. During start-up you need to choose a Range that includes some targets.

When navigating in restricted waters you have to be constantly aware of what information is relevant. This means that the Range may have to be adjusted frequently, using longer ranges to detect navigation marks and on-coming traffic and shorter ranges to examine the nearby surroundings.

One of the most common errors when navigating in restricted waters is to use too short a Range for too long a period. Although a knob is the easiest way to change Range, a plus/minus button is now more common.

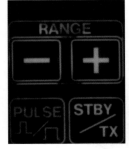

Types of Range controll.

In the picture below, information about the current Range is displayed on the far left. To the right of this is information about the distance between the range rings (see page 35). As this particular radar is interfaced with an electronic compass and a GPS, information about the course (from the electronic compass) and speed over ground (from the GPS) is also displayed.

Out in the open sea, radar is mostly operated on longer ranges to allow you to look for distant landmarks and ships, so there is not the same need for you to change the Range frequently. Closer inshore, there is a temptation to switch to shorter ranges. This is a good thing, in that it usually gives the clearest possible picture. But when the radar is switched to short ranges, it is important to remember that there may be unseen hazards just off the edge of the screen. The prudent navigator regularly takes a look at a longer range.

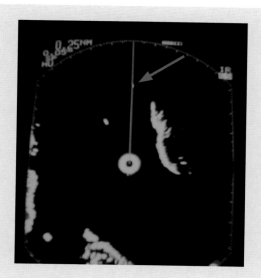

The Heading Mark starts from the centre of the picture and indicates the heading of the boat. It is always visible unless you delete it (with its spring-loaded button) in order to look for contacts hidden behind it. In the picture to the left, you can see a weak contact just to starboard of the Heading Mark.

Summary

To get a really clear picture, you may need to re-adjust all the controls again once the radar has warmed up completely. Radar sets from different manufacturers can react differently to the adjustment of the various controls. The Tune may need only minor adjustment on one radar and yet it can be quite crucial on another in order to get any picture at all. The same is true for Gain.

Radar sets are individual, and the process you go through to get a picture may differ between models. Some experienced users recommend making adjustments in alphabetical order – Brilliance, Gain, Range and Tune – but however you choose to do it, always remember:

- Start by turning Sea Clutter and Rain Clutter to zero.
- The screen needs you to adjust both Brilliance and Tune to show a picture.
- There must be sufficient Gain to amplify echoes.
- Objects must be within the Range to give contacts.
- Too much Sea Clutter can ruin the picture from the centre and outwards.

All the controls (Brilliance, Tune and Gain) are essential to get a good picture. Poor adjustment of any of them can ruin a picture, despite perfect adjustmant of the others.

Interpreting the picture

The radar may show a lot, while not telling you very much. Most objects in the vicinity will produce echoes but the strength of those echoes will vary depending on the object's size, shape, surface texture, the material it is made of, and the angle at which it is struck by the radar beam.

 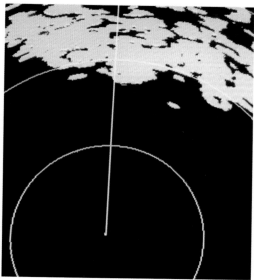

Buildings and breakwaters are very good radar targets. They are solid and have lots of irregularities that reflect radar pulses well.

The image of land on the radar screen does not look like the land as shown on the chart, and neither do the other contacts resemble things like ships and beacons. A contact on the screen only means that some sort of a target is reflecting the radar pulses.

In the open sea, a contact with no corresponding symbol on the chart is probably a ship or perhaps some other floating object. Along the coast a solitary contact could be a ship or a navigation mark such as a buoy. In restricted waters our expectations and prejudices may lead to mistakes between rocks and islands. A dinghy, a rock awash, a small floating navigational mark or a large bird swimming can all give a contact of about the same size. What shows up on the screen depends on the target, the distance and the adjustments of the radar.

Radar horizon

The radar can detect objects in darkness and mist, but it is not able to see beyond the 'radar horizon', where the shoreline and other low targets will not give any contacts. Luckily the radar horizon is slightly further away than the visual horizon.

The formula for the distance to the radar horizon is 2.2 x the square root of the height of the antenna.

For an antenna mounted 4 metres up a mast, the radar horizon is 4.4 miles away.

For the radar to be able to detect something beyond the radar horizon, the object has to be sufficiently high.

The distance at which an object might become visible on radar is given by the formula:

2.2 x √Height of antenna + 2.2 x √Height of target

So if the antenna is mounted at a height of 9 metres, a 100 metre cliff should start to appear at a range of about 6.6 + 22 = 28.6 miles

Raising the antenna provides only a minor effect. For example, raising the antenna from 4 metres to 9 metres will only increase the distance to the radar horizon from 4.4 miles to 6.6 miles.

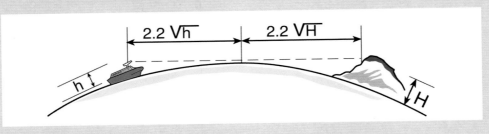

Refraction

Weather conditions may make the radar beam bend more or less, increasing or decreasing the distance to the radar horizon.

Sub-refraction occurs when the air temperature is colder than the sea temperature and this tends to reduce the distance to the radar horizon.

Super-refraction is the opposite. In fine weather and high pressure, when warm humid air is present over cold water, the radar beam will bend more than usual, following the surface of the earth. This increases the distance to the radar horizon.

In a phenomenon called 'ducting' the radar beam is reflected back and forth between layers in the atmosphere and the surface of the sea, so the range becomes even more extended.

Radar beam

For the radar to be able to register the
returning echo in the correct direction,
the pulses need to be sent in a narrow
arc: the narrower the better. This arc is
usually called the radar beam. Large radar
sets with long antennae can transmit within

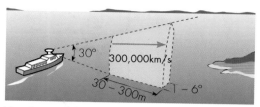

The shape of the radar pulse.

a sector covering less than one degree, while a small craft radar with a short antenna
transmits within an arc of 6 degrees. The vertical beam width is usually about 25-30
degrees, to ensure that when the boat rolls and pitches the beam still covers the targets.

Imagine a radar beam, six degrees wide, sweeping round the horizon like a beam of a
light. Any target will produce an echo when it is in the beam. This means that in the case
of a wide beam radar, the target will produce an echo while the scanner rotates through
six degrees, so the object will appear on the radar screen as a contact six degrees across.
By contrast, in the case of a narrow beam radar, the target will only be illuminated
during one degree of the scanner's rotation, so it will appear as a contact that is only one
degree across.

A harbour entrance, by contrast, will only show up when the radar beam is able to
pass straight through it, without being reflected by the land or breakwaters on each side.
So a harbour entrance that is 200 metres wide is likely to start appearing as a gap on a
radar with a 1 degree beamwidth at a range of about six miles, when it appears (by eye)
to be one degree wide. To a wide-beam radar, the gap will not appear to open until it is
six degrees wide, at a range of about one mile.

These two effects mean that the picture on a the screen of a wide-beam radar look
crude and blobby, which makes it more difficult to take accurate bearings than when
using a radar with a narrower beam.

A radar antenna revolves at about 20 to 50 rpm. A high-speed boat needs a fast
revolving antenna to minimise the delay in the picture.

Typical distortions of surroundings on
the radar screen.

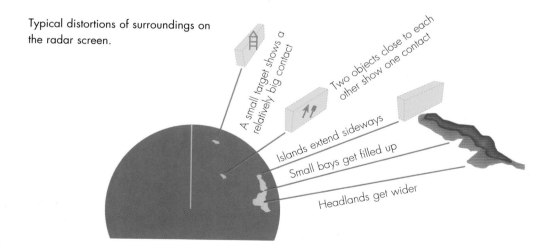

A small target shows a relatively big contact

Two objects close to each other show one contact

Islands extend sideways

Small bays get filled up

Headlands get wider

Pulse length

When the distance between two targets is less than the beam width at that spot, they appear to be only one contact.

Although the pulses transmitted by a radar are, in human terms, almost unimaginably short, each one still lasts for a definite, measurable period of time. This is usually somewhere between about one tenth of a microsecond (called a short pulse) and a whole microsecond (called a long pulse).

When a pulse first strikes a target it begins to produce an echo, and it goes on producing an echo for as long as the pulse goes on hitting it. So even a very small target such as a buoy will, when hit by a short pulse, produce an echo that lasts one tenth of a microsecond. This will elongate the contact on the radar screen so that the buoy appears to be about 15 metres long.

If the same buoy were hit by a long pulse, the contact produced by the same buoy would appear to stretch 150 metres!

This means that a radar using long pulses is unable to discriminate between objects that are on the same bearing and within 150 metres of each other, so a buoy lying just off a headland, for instance, will appear as an extension of the headland, rather than as a separate contact.

This means that short pulse lengths generally give a clearer, more accurate picture than long ones. Unfortunately, short pulses do not contain as much energy as long ones, so longer pulse lengths have to be used at longer ranges. On most small craft radars the pulse length is changed automatically to fit the range in use, but on a more sophisticated radar the operator is given at least some freedom of choice.

The radar cannot start detecting targets until its TR (Transmit/Receive) cell opens the path for echoes to travel from the antenna to the receiver. To protect the receiver, this must never happen until after the pulse has ended, so the minimum range at which targets can be detected is usually about 25 metres.

Sometimes, the minimum range may also be affected by electrical noise within the radar, producing the strong circular pattern that is clearly visible in the centre of the screen. This is called the Main Bang, and completely obscures real contacts.

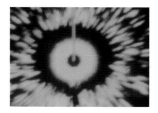

Some radar sets have a function called Target Expansion or Echo Stretch. What this actually does is make weaker contacts easier to see by artificially lengthening each contact, without making it any wider. You can see the effect of Echo Stretch on the contact in the upper part of the right-hand screen.

Radar shadow

The shorelines on the radar screen may only vaguely resemble those on the chart, as the radar will 'see' the surroundings from where the antenna is situated, but will show it as a picture seen from above. Anything hidden behind another target is invisible to the radar. On the chart below, you can see the position of the boat as the red dot. Compare the chart with the radar screen at the same moment.

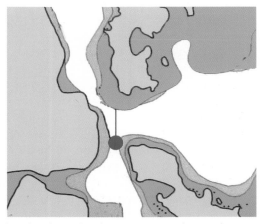

When interpreting the picture it is important to remember that the radar does not register lower objects behind the foreground. For this reason the shoreline is not continuous in the picture to the left.

For the same reason, the shape of the contact of an island may change as you pass by (see below). The long island ahead and to port gives a smaller contact when abeam.

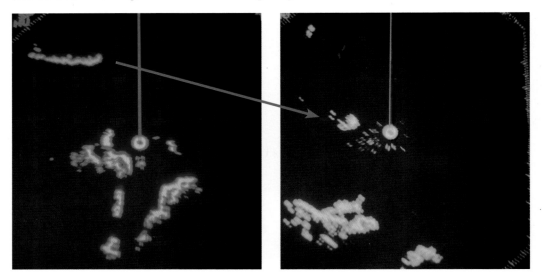

The quality of different targets

A large, flat, hard target, such as a ship or a building, will give a distinct echo when it is hit by a radar pulse at a right angle. When the same surface is hit by a radar pulse at another angle, much of the energy will be reflected in another direction and the contact will be weaker.

The intensity of a contact depends on:

- Size (usually the dominating factor): big is better.
- Height: high is better than low.
- Angle: normally a 90 degree angle to the surface is better than any other angle.
- Material: electrically conducting material is better than dielectric material.
- Surface structure: an uneven surface is better than a smooth surface.

Targets like ships, buildings and quays always show distinct contacts on the screen as they have lots of small irregularities.

A racon (see opposite page) is an active radar transponder which, when hit by a radar pulse, returns a signal on the same frequency. This appears on the radar screen as a Morse Code signal (dots and dashes) for the racon identification letter. The identification code also appears beside the racon symbol on the chart. The dashes are not shown continuously on the radar screen.

A racon.

Passive radar reflector on a buoy.

A passive radar reflector consists of flat surfaces at right-angles to each other. The pulses are reflected back to the radar antenna, no matter what the angle of incidence.

A tall cylindrical object (for example, a water tower or a chimney) gives a weak but consistent contact. Although a cylindrical object reflects much of the radar pulse away from the antenna, it will always show some narrow vertical surface directly facing it.

Big ships are excellent targets due to their large, hard surfaces and many small angles and corners, so they give good contacts at long range. In the picture below, on the left of the Heading Mark you can see a distinct contact from a big ship. Soft objects like waves and birds are poor targets, but at short range they will still be visible on the radar screen.

On the right you can clearly see the wash from a fast motorboat passing by.

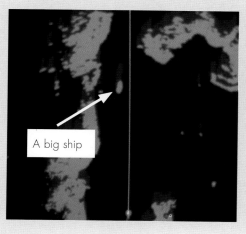

A big ship

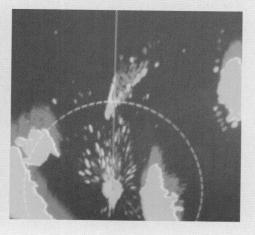

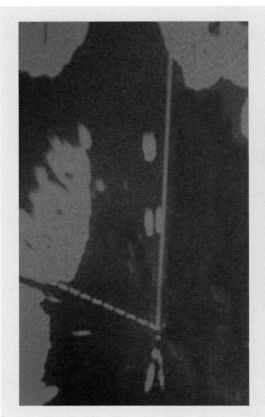

Left and above: Contacts from two large birds and, a little further away, a spar buoy. These contacts are extended radially by the length of the pulse.

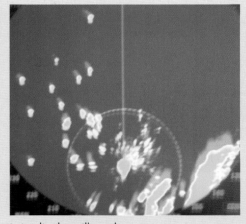

At close quarters, even objects as small as an Optimist dinghy will produce a contact.

Pontoons with
moored boats

Boats moored along
the shore

Own vessel

A false contact from
something onboard our
vessel

A bridge

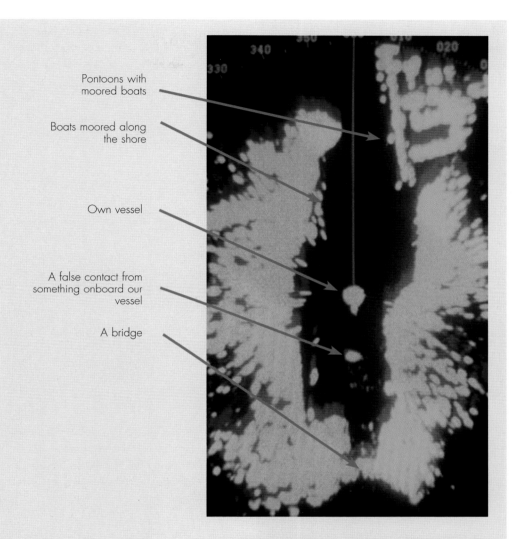

In the picture above you can see a screenshot from a radar with a long antenna. Such an antenna produces a narrow radar beam, so the contacts won't broaden as much as they would with a wide beam. The picture appears to be 'sharper'.

Small flat rocks are poor radar targets. Small targets reflect less of the radar pulse energy and when a pulse hits the target at angles other than 90 degrees, much of the reflected energy is directed away from the antenna. Increasing Gain slightly allows you to see an interesting yet weak target.

This picture (and the screenshots below) show four small targets at fairly close range: a small spar buoy, a tuft of grass, a rocky outcrop, and a rock awash.

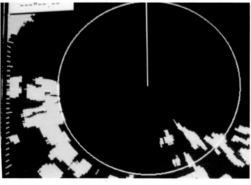

The targets are abeam to port. On this picture Gain is low. The vessel is moored to a quay on her starboard side. The distant shoreline to the left in the picture is the first target to give a contact.

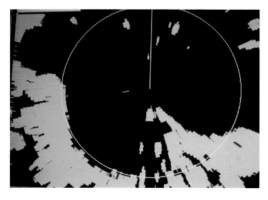

Here, Gain has been doubled. A small contact from a spar buoy appears abeam to port, with some sea clutter ahead.

In this picture Gain is still the same. Now there are two contacts abeam to port, but the spar buoy has disappeared. This behaviour is rather typical for contacts from spar buoys and other floating objects that are bobbing about in the waves.

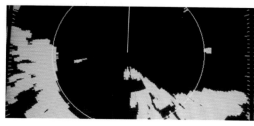

Even in this picture, Gain is the same, but now only one contact is visible on the port side. This contact comes from a tuft of grass. (The others are invisible in this image.) It is common for weak contacts to 'twinkle' like this.

Now Gain has been increased greatly and all the four contacts are visible. The shoreline behind the targets looks similar to that with little Gain, but the land contacts have merged.

This is the way that contacts of small objects or floating navigation marks behave on the radar screen.

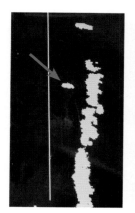 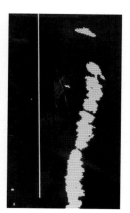 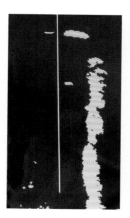 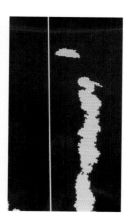

In these images you can see the 'twinkling' character of the contact of a buoy (see red arrow), at a distance of about 1 nautical mile. The more distant contact is from a ship, about 40 m in length, heading towards our vessel. Observe the slight side lobe contact (see p 24) from the ship in the first picture.

3 Disturbing phenomena

If you are close to land you may need to adjust the controls frequently, to obtain a picture that will:

- show what you want to see.
- not show what you do not want to see.

On the open sea when the radar is mostly working at longer ranges, the controls will not need to be adjusted as often. However, prudence demands a change to a shorter range at suitable intervals to investigate nearby objects. When you are trying to find a distant coastline or lighthouse you can increase the Gain strongly for a short time in order to get a glimpse of such a target.

Sea Clutter

The radar screen will almost always show intermittent contacts from nearby waves. This can be reduced with the Sea Clutter adjustment (also known as AC Sea 'Anticlutter Sea' or STC 'Sensitivity Time Control'). These can be either manual or automatic.

The Sea Clutter control also reduces other small contacts, so it should not be left in a position where it suppresses too much. It is therefore common practice to retain some sea clutter, so you have a more sensitive picture.

Gain and Sea Clutter interact with each other so you usually have to adjust them together: Sea Clutter is reduced

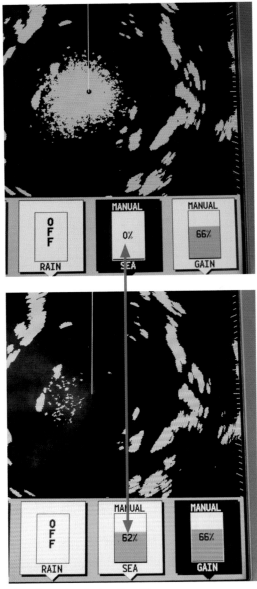

The effect of reducing Sea Clutter.

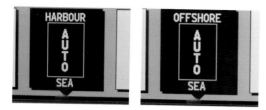

Two examples of automatic Sea Clutter, with different characteristics for harbour or offshore.

when Gain is reduced. The Sea Clutter control works by strongly suppressing contacts more in the centre of the screen than towards the periphery. When navigating close to land you can sometimes get a better picture by adjusting Sea Clutter rather than by decreasing Gain too much. Do not use automatic Sea Clutter without understanding how the picture will be influenced.

Rain Clutter

Raindrops are not good reflectors, but lots of them together can result in the characteristic pattern of Rain Clutter which will hide the contact of a more solid object. When the Rain Clutter control is activated, the radar cuts every returning echo so that only its leading part is displayed. With this setting activated, echoes of raindrops are too weak to produce contacts so the image you view is not as confused. You can see in the screenshots below that the land contacts are smaller, but the shoreline is sharper. Note also the target that was hidden by the rain. A control called FTC (Fast Time Constant) is available for suppressing heavy rain contacts at a longer range.

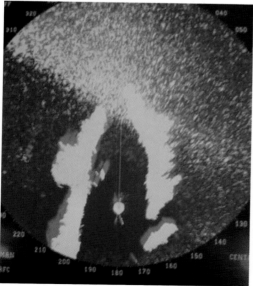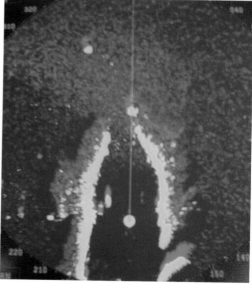

Notice how in the right screenshot the contact that was hidden by the rain is now clearly visible. It is also noticeable that the contacts from the land are smaller.

Side Lobe contacts

Every antenna leaks a small amount of energy outside the main radar beam. When passing close by a good target, Side Lobe contacts will appear on the screen. If these are distracting, temporarily decrease the Gain.

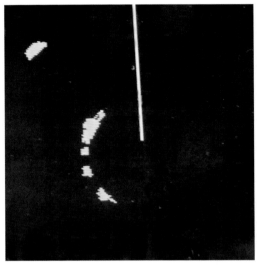

A contact with Side Lobe effect from a lighthouse with a radar reflector.

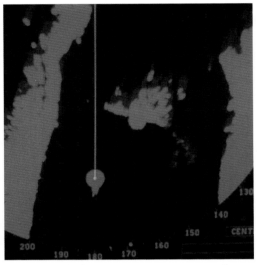

This strange-looking contact is an oncoming large ship at close range.

Indirect contacts

The radar pulse can be reflected by something aboard your own vessel or by some other target, and then be sent away in another direction. Under these circumstances the returning echo will be shown as coming from the wrong direction. Such 'ghost' contacts look slightly different from ordinary ones. Those which appear when reflected by other targets are only present for a short length of time, while those caused by reflection aboard will usually appear in the same place on the screen (at the arrow in the picture to the right). False or Indirect Contacts are usually obvious. If they confuse the image, decrease Gain.

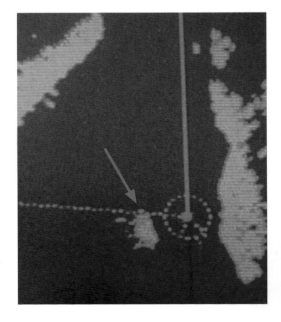

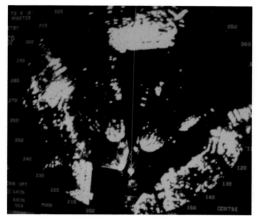 

The picture on the left shows a very distorted radar image with a number of contacts originating from pulses reflected by a big ship on the port side of our vessel. An absence of contacts in the upper left of the screen is caused by shadowing. The picture to the right shows the screen a bit later, after the ship and our vessel have moved apart.

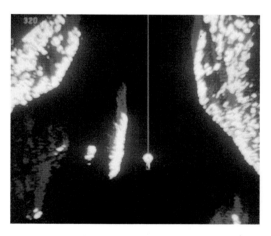

This picture shows the contact of a big ship as it passes close to port. To the left of the ship there are two 'multiple contacts' (ships). The pulse is bouncing to and fro between the ships and the contacts are being registered as new each time.

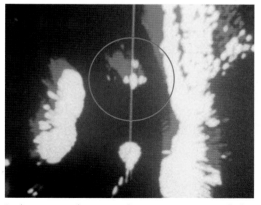

Power transmission lines will give a special kind of contact. Here, the line itself is too thin to return an echo, but the magnetic field around it will give a contact. When you start to close in on a power transmission line the contact appears to look like a little ferry just leaving the shore. No matter what you do, the ferry looks as if it is going to collide with you!

In this picture the power line contact is encircled.

Interference

Since different radar sets use more or less the same frequency, they may interfere with each other. The typical effect on your screen will appear as a series of dashed lines, sometimes radiating like the spokes of a wheel. The phenomenon is not very common and because it cannot be misunderstood, it does not present a problem. Nonetheless, most radar sets have a function called Interference Rejection (IR) which eliminates this effect. Because the effect of IR is essentially harmless, many navigators leave it on, but it has a tendency to reduce the background speckle which is important when adjusting Gain.

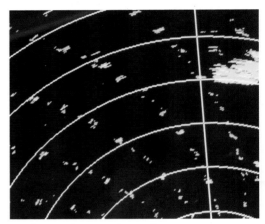

Interference from another radar.

Blind sectors

Blind sectors will appear if the antenna is mounted so that the pulses hit a part of your own vessel, such as the funnel or the mast. A thin mast may not necessarily lead to a fully developed blind sector, but the effect will still be reduced in that direction.

To determine if you have a blind arc, reduce Sea Clutter to zero on a day with significant sea clutter. Choose a Range in which the sea clutter reaches the edge of the screen. The arc in which the sea clutter is diminished shows the blind sector.

4

Display modes

Modern radar sets are able to present the picture in different modes, each one with advantages and disadvantages. 'Head-up' is the original mode and technically the simplest.

Head-up

This mode shows a picture with the Heading Mark pointing 'straight up' on the screen. Forward of the vessel corresponds to 'up' on the screen. The surroundings are presented with a relative motion. When your vessel is under way it appears to be stationary in the centre of the screen, and the contacts from fixed objects will move in a downward direction. Head-up presentation is particularly useful when navigating in restricted waters.

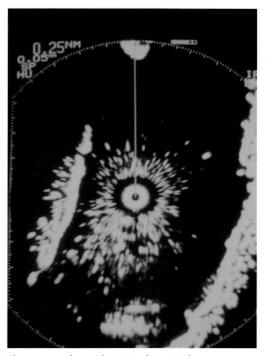

This screen shows the Heading Mark pointing 'straight up'. Forward of the vessel corresponds to 'up' on the screen.

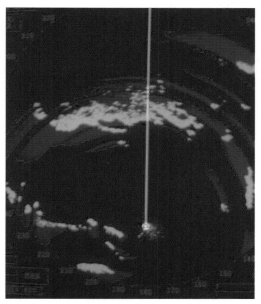

Head-up with relative motion during a turn. The whole picture is rotating but lagging behind, owing to the antenna's speed of rotation. The afterglow can be adjusted on modern radar sets. On old radar sets with CRT screens there is always some afterglow that cannot be removed.

The risk of collision with another vessel can be estimated in a similar way as when viewed by eye. A contact approaching on a steady bearing suggests that there is a risk of collision, but without extra work the Head-up presentation gives no information about the course and speed of the other vessel.

One drawback of this presentation mode is that the picture rotates as the vessel turns. Another is that bearings can only be measured directly if there is a compass interfaced to the radar, otherwise the heading has to be added to the direction observed with the radar.

Head-up is an 'unstabilized' mode in contrast to 'North-up' and 'Course-up', which are said to be 'stabilized'.

North-up

Using North-up solves two of the problems encountered with Head-up presentation: rotation of the image during turning and the difficulty in taking bearings. The radar needs to be interfaced to an electronic compass and to have computer software installed, which is able to turn the picture so that North is always up. In this mode the Heading Mark is pointing in the direction of the heading.

The advantages of this presentation are that the radar screen corresponds with the chart and the picture doesn't rotate. When the course is unsteady only the Heading Mark is moving and the picture remains stable, so the bearings are more easily determined.

However, not everyone likes to navigate with a Heading Mark pointing towards themselves when on a southerly course. Estimating the risk of collision is not made any easier, so North-up is not used much in confined waters but does very well for coastal navigation.

In North-up mode the Heading Mark points in the direction of the heading.

Course-up

Like North-up, this presentation needs the radar set to be interfaced to an electronic compass. The Heading Mark is pointing up, and the picture is stabilized. When the course is not steady, the Heading Mark will move to and fro. But with Course-up the picture itself remains steady and bearings are easily determined. After a deliberate turn the image needs to be reset, otherwise the Heading Mark will not point upwards.

All these types of presentation show 'relative motion'. Your vessel is stationary in the centre of the picture and, when under way, all fixed objects will move in the opposite direction relative to the Heading Mark.

Contacts from other moving ships will show a 'relative movement' which is a result of your own, and the other ships', movement.

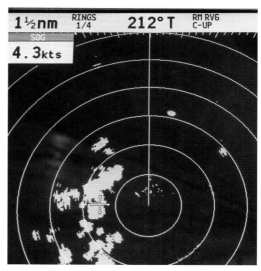

In Course-up mode your vessel is stationary in the centre of the picture.

Off centre

The 'Off centre' function allows the user maximum forward range on the screen. This is often desirable when navigating in confined waters.

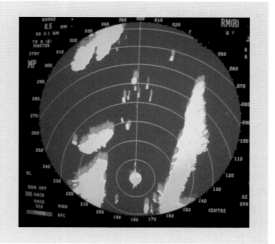

True Motion

In the 'True Motion' mode the position of your vessel is no longer fixed but moves with its own course and speed across the radar picture. Land and beacons remain stationary and other ships' movements are also presented with their course and speed. To achieve this the radar has to be interfaced to a positioning device, such as the GPS (ground stabilized true motion) or to a compass and a log (sea stabilized true motion). As your vessel is moving in the picture, the picture has to be moved back when the space ahead is too small.

True Motion gives information on the speed and course of other vessels, but it will not automatically give information on their relative bearing, which is vitally important when you have to determine the risk of collision.

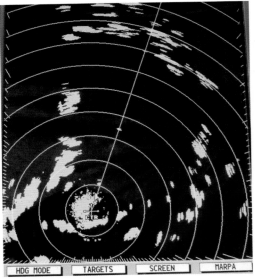 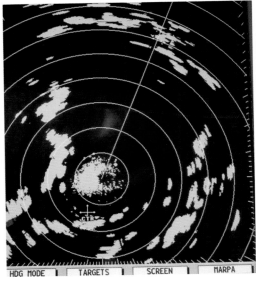

Our vessel moves in the radar picture in True Motion, North-up mode.

Radar Overlay

This function superimposes the radar picture over an electronic chart, making it easier for the navigator to identify islands and beacons. Contacts which do not correspond to anything on the electronic chart can be considered to be movable! This function demands a position source and a corrected compass in order to make the chart and the picture correspond exactly.

Using Radar Overlay is also an easy way to check if the GPS and the electronic charts are showing a correct position.

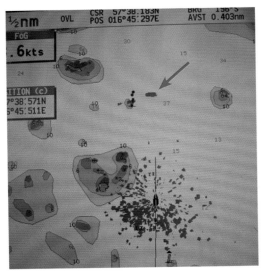

This radar picture is superimposed over an electronic chart. The contacts (violet) show the Sea Clutter around our vessel as well as contacts over a beacon and some small skerries. The contact marked by the red arrow is another vessel.

SOURCES OF TECHNICAL ERROR

A radar set builds up the picture on the screen by measuring distance and direction. The distance to an object is measured by the elapsed time between transmitting the pulse and receiving its echo. To check that the radar set measures distance correctly, observe the contact from an absolutely straight extended object, such as a quay or a bridge. If the echo on the screen is not a straight line, the set needs calibrating. Refer to the appropriate section of the owner's manual for instructions. If the radar antenna is not mounted in the correct direction, it will have a bearing error. Control this by steering straight towards a distinct object that gives a small, distinct echo, and compare with the Heading Mark direction. Adjust any alignment error according to the manual.

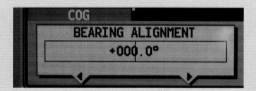

The window for correcting alignment error.

BROADBAND RADAR

The initials FMCW stand for Frequency Modulated Continuous Wave and refer to a technology that is new to small craft radar, known as Broadband Radar.

Like conventional marine radars, FMCW radars transmit microwave energy and receive the echoes that bounce back to their antennae. But instead of transmitting pulses that last less than 1 microsecond each (1 millionth of a second) an FMCW radar transmits 'sweeps' that last a millisecond each (one thousandth of a second).

In a conventional pulsed radar, switching from short pulse to long pulse packs more energy into each pulse, so it significantly increases the range at which any given target will produce a discernible echo. The ultra long pulses of FMCW have a similar effect, except that instead of increasing the range, it is used to reduce the transmitter power from several kilowatts to less than a watt.

In a conventional radar, increasing the pulse length from short pulse to long pulse reduces the radar's range discrimination. On that basis, the ultra-long pulses of FMCW are so long that they would be almost completely useless.

This problem is overcome by modulating the transmitter frequency, increasing it progressively throughout each sweep, before dropping back to its starting frequency for the beginning of the next sweep.

By the time the echo arrives back at the radar, the transmitted frequency has increased – so the received frequency is always lower than the transmitted frequency.

If the echo has come from a target at short range, the difference between the transmitter and receiver frequencies will be small. If the echo has come from a more distant target, the difference will be larger. It is frequency difference (rather than time) that is used to measure of the range of the target.

The combination of low power and the use of frequency modulation is claimed to give several significant benefits including:

- Lower energy consumption.
- Lower radiation from antenna.
- Better short-range resolution and discrimination.
- No tuning being required.
- No warming up time.
- Better sea clutter rejection.

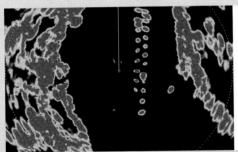

The picture on the left is an image from a Broadband radar, compared to an image from a pulse radar on the right.

HD-radar

HD-radar sends the same type of energy as an ordinary pulsed radar, but the reflected pulse is digitized as it comes back. The digitized pulse is analyzed by the radar's software, which creates a sharper image.

Part 2
Navigation

5

Navigating by radar

The ability of radar to give you a bird's-eye view of your situation, similar to the chart perspective, is very useful in clear weather as well as in fog. Using radar makes it possible to steer towards a headland or a bay and detect small islands that to the naked eye seem to merge together with the background. However, radar is at its most useful when navigating at night or in fog, providing the navigator with information that no other single instrument can deliver.

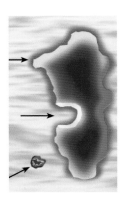

Some natural features to aim for, especially suitable for radar navigation.

Navigating by radar close to land or in confined waters involves following an intended track, checking the actual position and correcting the heading when the vessel is not on the intended track. (It is not always necessary to obtain a fix as a point on the chart, but this should of course be carried out when the situation is tight.)

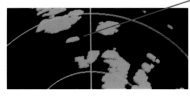

On the radar you can see some small islands or reefs that are otherwise almost invisible against the background.

Navigation in general is a continuous process of solving the following two problems:

1 'What is my position?'
2 'In which direction should I steer?'

Radar navigation provides the opportunity to work repeatedly with the two problems. When the first problem has been solved, you proceed to the second. Then you are back to the first problem again, as a check.

Identifying your position

Range

Because of the width of its beam, radar is a better tool for measuring range than for measuring bearing, so navigators generally prefer to use range-measuring to determine a fix. However, a distinct and clearly identified target is always needed. The chart shows two shorelines: Chart Datum, which is the lowest predicted tide level, and Mean High Water Springs (where green meets yellow). Intervening positions of the shoreline have to be guessed at, so the question is 'Does the tide influence the distance to a target right now?' If the coastline is steep the range will not be affected and the same is true for buoys and fixed sea marks. The contact may be better defined if the Gain is reduced slightly while you measure.

The simplest way to measure range is to use the Fixed Range Rings. You can switch these on and off, and on some sets you will be able to adjust their intensity. On modern radar sets you can also read, somewhere on the screen, the distance between the rings. On older radars those figures are written beside the range button.

A more accurate result is obtained using the Variable Range Marker (VRM) and there are usually two VRMs. On modern radar sets there may also be a third method, known as 'Cursor': this measures range and bearing simultaneously and shows the result on the screen.

The position line resulting from one measured range will be a circle on the chart. Two ranges will give two possible positions (see below). Navigating in confined waters is a continuous process, with consecutive positions close to each other – the wrong positions are quickly identified. The most convenient way to draw the range circles on the chart is to use a pair of compasses with a lead tip at one end.

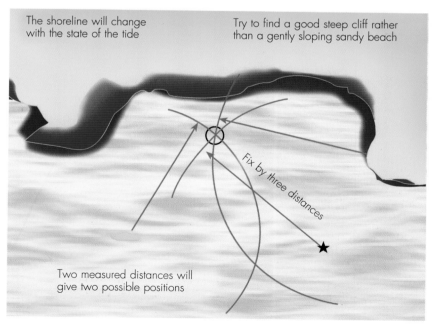

The shoreline will change with the state of the tide

Try to find a good steep cliff rather than a gently sloping sandy beach

Fix by three distances

Two measured distances will give two possible positions

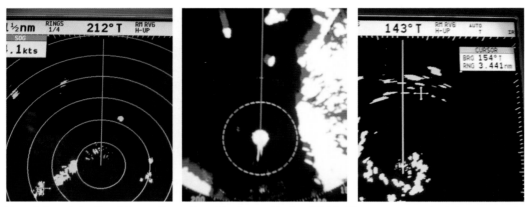

From left to right: Fixed Range Rings. Variable Range Marker (VRM). The cursor gives both bearing and range, as shown in the box ('T' after 'degrees' stands for 'True').

Determining direction

Most radars are equipped with one or two Electronic Bearing Lines (EBLs), which can be moved around the screen by means of a control on the operator's panel. When the Electronic Bearing Line is positioned so that it cuts through a contact on the screen, the bearing of that contact is displayed in a data panel, usually in one corner of the screen.

Unless some kind of electronic compass is supplying the radar with information about which direction the boat is heading, the radar can only display a relative bearing – a direction measured relative to the vessel's heading. For most purposes it needs to be converted to a true bearing by adding the compass course, and adding or subtracting the variation and deviation.

Suppose, for instance, that the EBL displays a bearing of 296°. The boat's heading (compass) is 150°, the deviation is 3°E and the variation is 4°W.

Relative bearing	296	
Compass heading	150	Add the compass heading of the boat
Compass bearing	446	
Deviation	+ 3	Always add easterly compass errors when converting to True
Magnetic bearing	449	
Variation	– 4	
True bearing	445	
	360	Subtract 360° if required
True bearing	085	

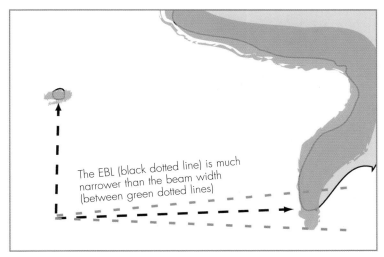

The EBL (black dotted line) is much narrower than the beam width (shown by the green dotted lines).

The accuracy of the whole calculation depends on the accuracy with which the helmsman is holding his course, but there is plenty of scope for arithmetical errors as well. It is much better to connect the radar to an electronic compass so that the EBL can give a compass bearing. Even then, though, the accuracy of a bearing measured by small craft radar, with its rather short antenna and comparatively wide radar beam, is unlikely to be good.

In the illustration above, the radar contact of the land is superimposed on the chart. The contact of the little island is elongated in both directions. Place the EBL in the centre of such a contact. When taking a bearing to the headland, you have to choose between:

1 Placing the EBL half a beam width inside the outer edge of the contact.
2 Placing the EBL on the outer edge of the contact and subtracting half the beam width from the reading.

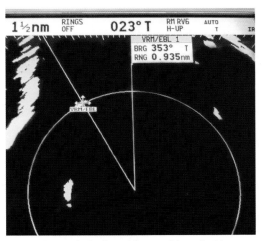

If only one contact is visible on the screen, a fix can be obtained by measuring bearing and range. Even the combination of a radar range measurement with a visual bearing can be very useful.

Bearing and range to a single object are seldom used for a fix in confined waters, but can be useful in coastal navigation.

In addition to making fixes, the combination of EBL and VRM is useful for identifying new contacts.

EBL and VRM linked together and handled by the cursor. Bearing (BRG) and range (RNG) are displayed in the box.

PLANNING AHEAD

Having a plan for navigating by radar in confined waters, with intended tracks, compass-courses, distances, landmarks etc, will give you a great deal of comfort when the fog rolls in. There will still be a lot to do: adjusting the controls of the radar, identifying contacts on the screen, comparing the screen with the chart, watching out for moving targets and monitoring the risk of collision.

For the single-hander navigating with radar in fog, it is of vital importance to keep a straight course between waypoints. If you're concentrating on a specific part of the radar image (perhaps studying some contacts and wondering what they represent) the boat can all too easily drift from her course without your noticing! What starts out as a little deviation can end up as a large error before you realize what is going on. In such conditions use the autopilot if you have one.

The first step when planning a trip is to choose the route, taking into account depth, dangers to navigation, clearance under bridges, weather conditions and so on. Choose features to aim for, find reference targets to define waypoints (ranges, buoys, bearings) and distances abeam for course control. GPS and electronic charts will also support you when solving some of these problems.

You can concentrate more on operating the radar at the time by drawing and measuring useful courses and ranges in advance. But if the chart hasn't been prepared in advance, you can still work through the problems as the text and picture below shows.

Draw the course line with adequate margins for danger areas. It is a good idea to draw the course to the starboard side in fairways where on-coming traffic is expected. Turning, especially through large angles, has to be planned well in advance. When making a large turn at high speed, use a good compass to point out the new leg and then check it against the radar. (The Heading Mark will be too slow to be useful during the turn.)

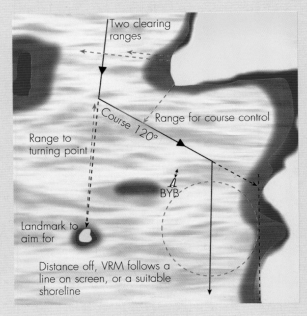

Two clearing ranges

Course 120°

Range for course control

Range to turning point

BYB

Landmark to aim for

Distance off, VRM follows a line on screen, or a suitable shoreline

6 Pilotage

It is not always necessary to know exactly where you are, as long as you know that you are not in the wrong place. The radar is very useful for guiding you along a route, without determining your exact position. After planning the journey and preparing the chart, follow your plan. It is best to do the preparation in advance, which avoids having to do the necessary measurements during the voyage.

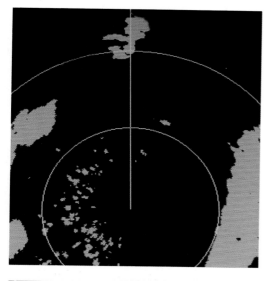

When aiming at a small object such as an island, the Heading Mark is a good guide.

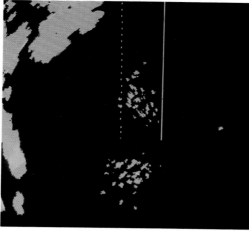

If there is no landmark dead ahead, the Floating EBL can be used as a steering guide.

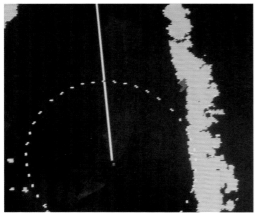

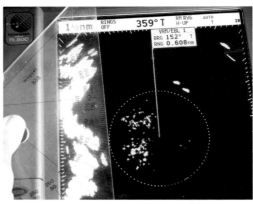

This track can be controlled by using the VRM to follow a straight shoreline. This is a kind of parallel indexing, further dealt with on page 44.

Distance off when the shoreline isn't straight. Put a ruler or something with a straight edge along identified points on the screen and let the VRM guide you by following that edge.

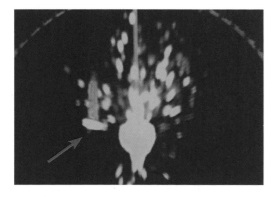

The Wake, Trail, Tail, or Track function can be used to highlight automatically the apparent movement of contacts on the screen. To the left you can see a tail on the contact from a buoy passing close to port.

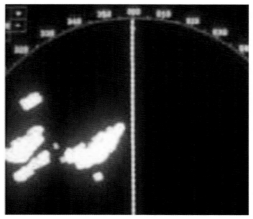

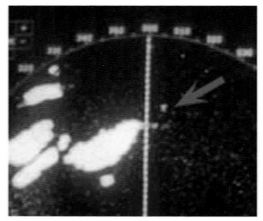

Even for targets at short range, there are reasons to adjust the Gain. To the left is a good image and contacts with sharp shorlines. To the right, more Gain reveals a contact from a small spar buoy (see arrow).

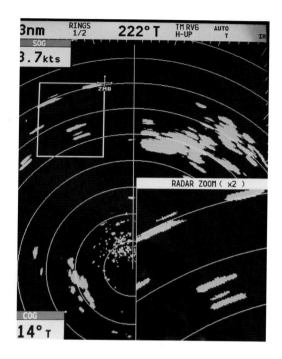

Contacts of small objects at a distance, which will not be seen on a shorter and more distinct Range, can be enlarged using the Zoom function and displayed in a part of the screen (in this picture, in the lower right corner of the screen).

WORKING WITH THE PICTURE

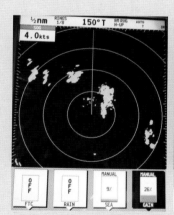
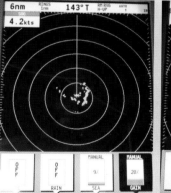

Use low Gain when close to land, in order to have sharp shorelines.

Emerging from a sound. In the left-hand picture, Gain is too low; adjustment will not reveal distant contacts. To the right, more Gain shows information at longer ranges.

Controlling your track

If you are in a narrow channel or have a navigational aid nearby it is possible to check that the vessel is following the intended course by measuring the range to an object abeam. When there is nothing measurable abeam, the position can be fixed by using at least two range readings. When the vessel is in a crosswind or there is a cross-current there will be a sideways force called 'set', and it is important to take this effect into account.

Aiming for a target dead ahead is no guarantee that you will arrive there along the planned course. When just aiming for a contact on the radar, the set will not be obvious. Monitor your compass course or course over Ground (COG) with the GPS. If the compass course changes while you are still aiming at the same contact, or if the COG according to the GPS differs from the course of the planned track, then you have an indication that there is set.

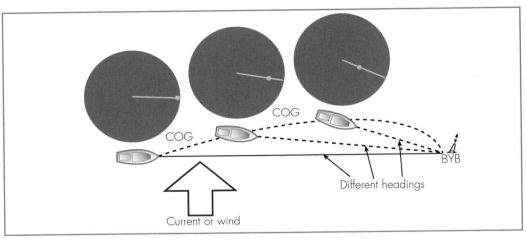

Aiming for a contact.

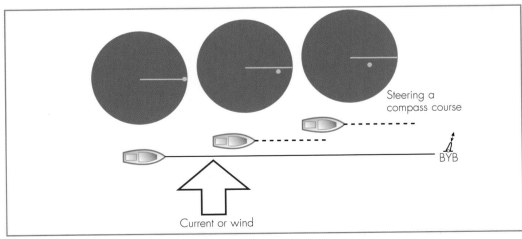

Same heading, but the contact is not following the Heading Mark.

The Trail function (also referred to as Wake, Tail etc) is another way to investigate the effect of set. This function keeps contacts in the memory for a predefined period, creating a 'trail' on the contact. When the trail of a fixed object is not parallel to the Heading Mark, and you are steering a steady course, it is a sign of set.

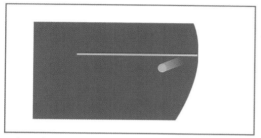

When the Trail of a fixed object isn't parallel to the Heading Line, it is a sign of set.

Once set has been detected, apply compensation to counteract it. When the amount of compensation is known, the EBL can be used for aiming towards a specific contact.

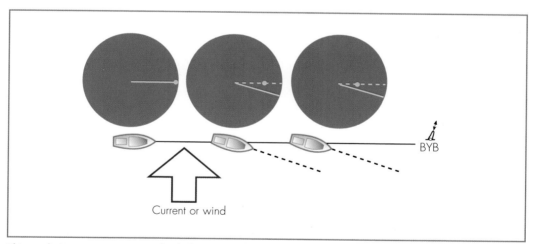

This yacht is compensating perfectly for set, and progressing straight for the buoy.

Parallel indexing

Parallel indexing is a special technique that helps the vessel keep to an intended track. It uses the principle that it is possible to predict the way a fixed object will appear to move on the radar screen. The procedure is as follows.

On the chart:
1 Plot the intended track as straight lines (A–C and C–D in the diagram below).
2 Choose a conspicuous feature as an 'index mark' (the north-western tip of the island).
3 Measure the shortest distance from the index mark to the first leg of the intended track (the red dotted line) and note whether the track is (roughly) north, south, east or west of the index mark.
4 Note the direction of the intended track.

On the radar screen:
5 Set the Variable Range Marker (VRM) to the distance measured in step 3.
6 Draw a line on the screen, in the direction corresponding to the direction of the intended track (from step 4), just touching the VRM. One handy method, on some radars, is to use a function called the 'floating EBL' to draw an electronic line on the display: another option is to use a grease pencil or white-board marker on the screen itself.
7 Check that the line passes the correct side of the centre of the screen: in the diagram, for example, the first leg of the track (A–C) passes to the west of the island, so the island should pass to the east of the centre of the screen.
8 Repeat steps 3–7 for the next leg of the intended track (C–D).
9 Steer so that the contact representing the index mark follows the lines drawn on the screen.

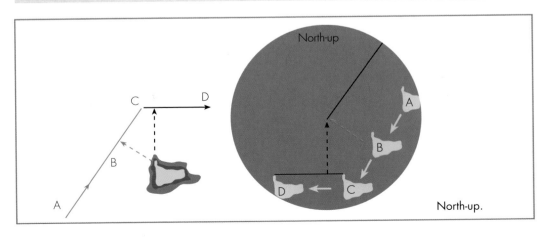

North-up.

Altering course

Parallel indexing is a particularly powerful tool for identify the right moment to alter course (the 'wheel over mark') to find an inconspicuous harbour entrance.

In the diagram below, for instance, the harbour entrance will not show up on the radar, but there is a conspicuous isolated island just along the coast.

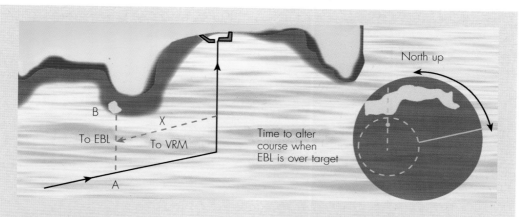

On the chart:

1 Draw the intended tracks (black lines).
2 Draw a line AB parallel to the intended second track, passing through the chosen wheel-over mark (in this case, the isolated island).
3 Measure the distance X between the intended track and the line passing through the wheel-over mark.

On the radar screen:

4 Ensure that the radar is in North-up mode.
5 Set the floating VRM to the distance X between the intended track and the wheel-over mark (measured in step 3).
6 Set the floating EBL to the direction of the intended track.
7 Move the floating EBL so that it just brushes the VRM.
8 Alter course when the wheel-over mark (the island) touches the floating EBL, then steer to keep the wheel-over mark sliding along the floating EBL.

CLEARING RANGES

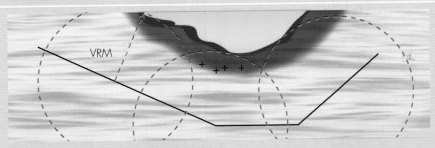

Here another vessel is guided by the VRM to clear a headland safely.

If you know that there are no hazards beyond a certain distance from the coast, then it is easy to avoid them by setting the VRM to a very slightly greater distance — known as the clearing range — and then making sure that the coastline does not appear inside the VRM.

Because this technique does not involve measuring direction, it can be used equally well in Head-up or North-up mode.

Stopping in time

A major challenge when navigating in restricted visibility is not to overshoot when trying to enter a narrow entrance or arrive at a landing place. Provided that the contact is from the correct target, the easiest way to reach a successful result is to position the vessel several hundred metres off the target and then steer straight in, as long as there is no current! (Obviously if there is a strong or weak current it is more difficult and you mustn't forget that the more you decrease your speed, the more the current will influence COG.)

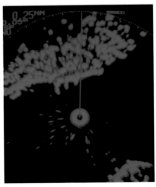

In this screenshot there is about 150 metres to the quay: You can work this out by checking the range information in the upper left corner of the screen.

Judging the distance ahead using radar can be difficult. The radar screen will not give the same feeling of distance as you get when seeing your landing place getting bigger before your eyes. If you reduce speed gradually, the radar can very easily create the impression that the remaining distance is greater than it really is.

On your way towards the target, the distance shortens and you need to adjust the Range. Set a VRM – for example at 200 metres – to remind you of the scale. Don't think of the remaining distance as 'half a screen' – think of it in metres instead. If the goal isn't visible at 200 metres, proceed very slowly indeed!

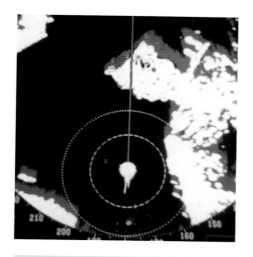

Two VRM are used as markers of risk areas – the outer one for movable targets, and the inner one for fixed targets. How they should be positioned depends on the vessel's manoeuvrability and the surroundings.

IDENTIFYING OBJECTS

During a voyage new contacts will continually come into view in the upper part of the screen (if you're in Head-up mode). Islands, beacons and buoys have to be identified before they can be used for navigation. This is best done with the aid of range and direction from your present position (or bearing, if the radar is connected to a reliable compass) and the shape and position of the contact in comparison with previously identified objects.

Ranges are measured by fixed range rings or the VRM. Direction or bearing is measured by the EBL. Draw the results on the chart measuring from your actual position, and the new echoes will be identified.

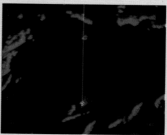

Left: From a reliable fix, measure the range and direction/bearing to unidentified objects.
Right: When emerging from confined waters onto the open sea, an entirely different image will appear on the screen. An easily recognised island, such as the one on the Heading Mark, makes a good reference point. The floating EBL and the VRM can be used to check the identity of an unknown object by measuring its range and bearing from one that has already been identified.

A very useful technique for identifying new objects is to transfer a waypoint from the electronic chart (placed with the GoTo function, for example). See photo on right.

Another useful identification technique is shown on the screenshot below. On the right of this particular radar screen a simple electronic chart (e-chart) is showing only the shoreline. The left part of the screen displays the full e-chart, and the radar screen cursor is coupled with the cursor of the e-chart. By pointing at a contact on the radar screen, the e-chart will reveal if it is a floating object or not. As an added benefit this radar shows in red all contacts with no counterpart on the e-chart.

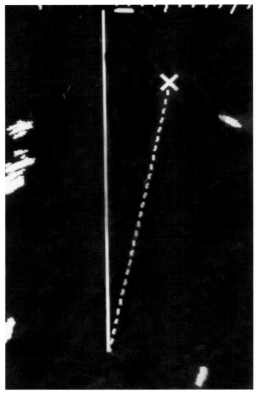

This waypoint on the radar screen was initially plotted on the electronic chart.

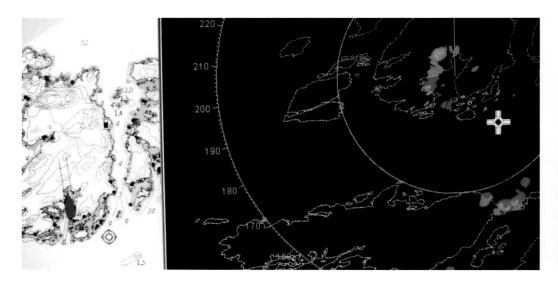

THE HUMAN FACTOR

As discussed at the start of the first chapter, radar can show you a lot, but tell you very little. There are many traps for the unwary. A person who is overconfident because they are familiar with the area or the situation runs the risk of overestimating their ability if their knowledge is actually not up to date.

Unusual incidents can easily increase the risk in a situation. For example, if forced away from the planned track by the weather, or the chance of a collision, the skipper must be sure that the depth of water on the new track is adequate (this is a risk independent of navigation method).

A large alteration of course, using radar in Head-up mode, within narrow passages and in darkness or restricted visibility, is far more difficult than the same manoeuvre in clear weather. On a clear day it is easy to judge the rate of turn, using the relative movement of the stem against the background. In restricted visibility, the navigator is looking down at a rotating radar image (if using Head-up) that lags behind the rate of turn. This is very different from a visual appraisal of the situation, and the turn can easily start too late and be too wide.

A bigger turn is even more difficult to handle. It demands a larger rudder angle, which increases the risk of over-compensation and an s-shaped wake. The boat is moving forward all the time, and the radar picture will rotate even more while still lagging behind, and the control over the situation diminishes. Avoid this by starting the turn early and, if it is going to be really big, reduce your speed before turning.

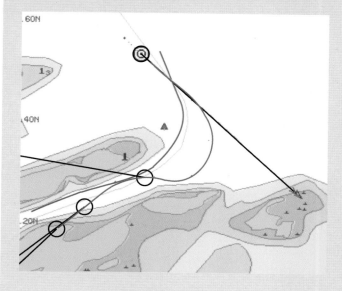

A real-life situation. The boat followed the red line, and ended up ashore at 30 knots. The delay of radar and e-chart images could have contributed to the accident. The green route would have been easier to follow. The circle at the boat's positions is about 30 m. (© The Swedish Board of Investigation.)

A radar screen is poor at giving an accurate impression of range. When navigating visually, a scene is full of information about range, because trees look smaller at a distance, islands far away look hazier and so on. When navigating with radar in confined waters or close to land, frequent changes to the Range scale are normal, and it is easy to lose track of what Range scale the radar is actually working on. For this reason it is important to check the displayed Range scale continually on the screen, and place a VRM as a reminder, especially when using shorter ranges.

Another thing to watch out for is your own knowledge about the limitations of radar (such as radar shadow and bad target quality) misleading you into interpreting the picture in the wrong way, and accepting a picture which in fact is not really correct! 'That little island probably won't show up at this distance, as it's small, low, wet and sloping.' 'It is lying in the radar-shadow.' 'It is hidden by the sea clutter.' 'That sparbuoy will probably give too weak an echo', etc.

- Look for information that will reveal faults and mistakes.
- Continue to work with the control settings on the radar to get a better image.
- Measure distances and bearings between different targets on the screen in order to make sure your identifications are correct.
- Look out for characteristic formations, such as groups of islands.

Making landfall

Out on the open sea, radar is valuable for avoiding collisions (see Part Three) and navigation is mainly achieved by other means, preferably including a GPS and e-charts. As a vessel moves closer to the coast, contacts will start to appear on the radar screen, but they will not look very much like the corresponding shoreline on the chart. Usually the first contacts from a distant coast look like islands, because the highest points give the first contacts. The beam width will fill in, round out, and distort the contacts. For the first observations, increase Gain, turn on Echo Stretch and if it can be adjusted use the longest possible pulse.

Once the shoreline is being shown accurately it is possible to start measuring ranges and bearings. Because of the beam width, bearings made at long range are not very accurate, but high accuracy is not needed when no dangers are close by. Ideally a radar range should be combined with a visual bearing.

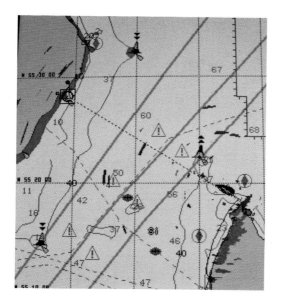

The first contacts from the highest points of land ahead (in magenta) at a distance of about 20 miles on an electronic chart with radar overlay.

Summary

Practical radar navigation is a continuous activity involving:

1 Position fixing and/or avoiding 'no go areas'.
2 Controlling the course (i.e. using fixes or clearing ranges in relation to the intended course).
3 Detecting the set caused by wind and/or current.
4 Identifying new echoes on the screen.
5 Altering and checking courses.

Remember: the difference between a skipper who runs aground and one who doesn't is often that the latter discovers their mistake in time!

Part 3

Collision avoidance in restricted visibility

Proceeding with caution

When you can see another vessel in clear visibility, you can usually distinguish:

- What type of vessel it is.
- Whether there is a risk of collision.
- Whether your own manoeuvre will be sufficient to prevent collision.

You may also be able to make a reasonable estimate of:

- Its heading.
- Its speed.
- Whether it is changing course and/or speed.

In restricted visibility you will have to make all these observations using your radar. When navigating by radar in confined waters in fog, you will often find that new contacts suddenly appear on the screen. Perhaps you have just changed the Range or made some other adjustment to the set, or the new contact has just appeared from behind a headland.

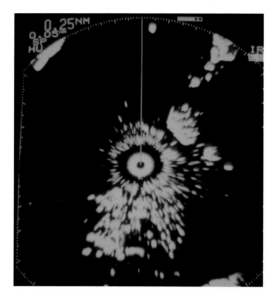

A Contact has suddenly appeared at the top of the screen to the right of the Heading Mark. At this time all you know is that something is there. With the radar set to such a short range as this there is no time to make a proper assessment of the situation: that is why Rule 7 of the collision regulations insists on the need for 'long range scanning'.

When you first see a contact you won't necessarily know what it is, so you will need to study it for some time before making a tentative identification. Even more time will pass before you can get a good idea of its heading. So while a visual look-out on deck in good visibility gives you present-time information, using the radar screen in fog means you are working with information that is already in the past. And as this information is not immediately understandable, you will need time to interpret it.

Every meeting between two vessels consists of four phases:

1 Discovery of the other vessel.
2 Evaluating the risk of collision.
3 Taking action to avoid collision.
4 Following up the effects of the avoiding action.

In comparison with clear weather, in restricted visibility every phase has to be handled very differently.

The importance of a look-out in restricted visibility

Rule 5. Every vessel shall at all times maintain a proper look-out by sight and hearing as well as by all available means appropriate in the prevailing circumstances and conditions so as to make a full appraisal of the situation and of the risk of collision.
(Note: Rules in these yellow boxes are taken from the Colregs.)

In restricted visibility, a dedicated look-out is invaluable.

The need to keep a sharp look-out is not lessened by the use of radar. On the contrary, it increases because safe radar handling really requires a dedicated operator whose job is to monitor and interpret the radar image continuously as it develops over time. For the same person to alternate between visual look-out and radar observation increases the risk of missing something from one of these sources. If it is unavoidable that one person has to carry out both jobs, then the speed of the vessel should be reduced as much as the situation demands. In many investigations into collisions in fog, a criticism has been the lack of an appropriate look-out on both vessels.

The best arrangement is for the skipper to concentrate on radar observation and feed the information to the look-out, who can adjust his work pattern accordingly. If you have an autopilot, use it. When the look-out reports a visual contact (ship, beacon, or land) the skipper can change to manoeuvring the vessel using visual information.

Finding a safe speed

Rule 6. Every vessel shall at all times proceed at a safe speed so that she can take proper and effective action to avoid collision and be stopped within a distance appropriate to the prevailing circumstances and conditions.

Nowadays the Colregs demand a 'safe speed' in both clear and restricted visibility. Taking into account all the different factors involved, including the size of vessels, it is not surprising that 'safe speed' cannot be defined in knots. Rules 6 a) and b) list some of the factors that have to be considered when determining what constitutes a 'safe speed'. Please note that the list is not necessarily exhaustive, nor is it set out in order of priority.

In determining a safe speed, the following factors are among those taken into account:

Rule 6 (a) By all vessels:
(i) the state of visibility;
(ii) the traffic density including concentrations of fishing vessels or any other vessels;
(iii) the manoeuvrability of the vessel with special reference to stopping distance and turning ability in the prevailing conditions;
(iv) at night, the presence of background light such as from shore lights or from back scatter of her own lights;
(v) the state of wind, sea and current, and the proximity of navigational hazards;
(vi) the draft in relation to the available depth of water.

Rule 6 (b) Additionally, by vessels with operational radar:
(i) the characteristics, efficiency and limitations of the radar equipment;
(ii) any constraints imposed by the radar range scale in use;
(iii) the effect on radar detection of the sea state, weather and other sources of interference;
(iv) the possibility that small vessels, ice and other floating objects may not be detected by radar at an adequate range;
(v) the number, location and movement of vessels detected by radar;
(vi) the more exact assessment of the visibility that may be possible when radar is used to determine the range of vessels or other objects in the vicinity.

Therefore, when navigating in confined waters and restricted visibility, you must continually be aware of how the situation is developing with regard to the risks around you. You must be ready to take immediate action to adjust your speed and/or course, to maintain an adequate safety margin around your vessel. Approximately 60% of all collisions in restricted visibility are said to involve excessive speed.

Although it isn't possible to set out hard and fast rules as to what a 'safe speed' is, the rules used to use the expression 'moderate speed', with the definition that a vessel ought to be able to stop within half of the range of visibility. This is still an appropriate definition of 'safe speed' for small vessels.

But in order to be able to stop within half the range of visibility, you must allow for your ability to detect other vessels and your own reaction time. You also need an extra safety margin for mistakes and technical faults. The safety margin for fixed targets should be doubled for moving targets from ahead but can be relaxed somewhat for moving targets approaching from astern. It is a good idea to place one or two VRMs to mark your safety margin (see also pages 47 and 58).

The combination of fog and darkness requires the utmost caution. In these circumstances, visibility may be 20–30 metres and a searchlight is of very little help until the target is very close. In confined waters the situation is changing continuously; other vessels may appear suddenly and alter course equally quickly and there is always the danger of shoals nearby.

The cautious radar navigator should be prepared to reassess his decisions frequently, as a heading that seems to be safe at the moment may soon become dangerous. This is particularly important when trying to monitor the risk of collision.

The conduct of vessels in restricted visibility is governed by Rule 19, which states:

Rule 19

(a) This Rule applies to vessels not in sight of one another when navigating in or near an area of restricted visibility.

(b) Every vessel shall proceed at a safe speed adapted to the prevailing circumstances and conditions of restricted visibility. A power-driven vessel shall have her engines ready for immediate manoeuvre.

(c) Every vessel shall have due regard to the prevailing circumstances and conditions of restricted visibility when complying with the Rules of Section I of this Part.

(Note: Rules of Section 1 deal with: Conduct of vessels in any condition of visibility, lookout, risk of collision, action to avoid collision, narrow channels, traffic separation schemes.)

Summary

When fog is imminent, you should immediately:
- establish a good look-out.
- slow down to a safe speed.
- use a fog signal and navigation lights.

8

Locating and monitoring moving targets

In confined waters, amidst normal or heavy traffic, it is not easy even for a trained operator to determine whether a contact represents a moving target or not. In your navigation work you are constantly interpreting the radar image and comparing it with the chart. A contact with no counterpart on the chart must be considered to be moving.

You also need to look at contacts in relation to each other. When two contacts diverge, at least one of them has to be moving. You need to be very vigilant in this kind of work: the contact from a small boat could merge with the contact of the land. If the boat suddenly changes course it may unexpectedly reappear on the screen, when you were under the impression that the only contact on that side was from the shore!

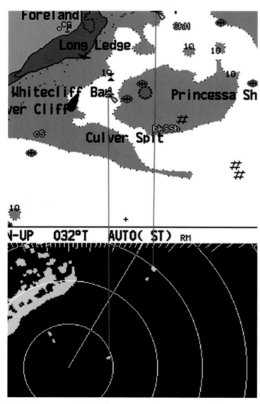

Both these contacts have counterparts on the chart.

Guard Zones

Modern radar sets have a function called Guard Zones. These can be set up as a circle round the vessel or, using the cursor, as a sector-shaped zone (see screenshot below). The inner guard border is situated at some distance from your own vessel so as not to react to sea clutter. The radar will then react to all contacts that enter the Guard Zone.

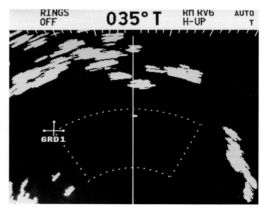

The Guard Zone has been set within the dotted lines.

Trail function

The Trail function (also known as the Tail or Wake function) is found on most modern radars and helps users to detect moving contacts. When activated, the radar screen creates a 'picture memory'. All contacts which are moving on the screen will produce a trail. Different movements produce different trails. In non-tidal waters, fixed and non-moving contacts have trails which are parallel to the Heading Mark. Moving targets produce trails of different shapes. A contact with no trail, for instance, is a target moving in the same direction, and at the same speed as your own vessel. But when your own vessel is yawing or altering course, the trails will become 'worms': they become zig-zagged or 'wriggly', and are more difficult to interpret.

The length of the memory (and therefore length of trails) is adjustable.

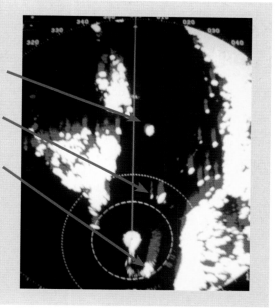

These trails show:

1. A ship with the same course and speed as your own vessel (no trail).

2. A beacon, with a buoy between it and the Heading Mark (parallel trails).

3. A contact from an oncoming vessel just passing to starboard (longer trail).

All contacts with trails different from number 2 are from moving targets.

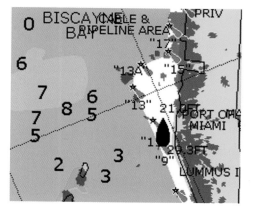

An e-chart with radar overlay. A contact with no counterpart on the e-chart is considered to be a movable target.

9

Assessing the risk of collision

The Colregs state that:

Rule 7
(a) Every vessel shall use all available means appropriate to the prevailing circumstances and conditions to determine if risk of collision exists. If there is any doubt such risk shall be deemed to exist.
(b) Proper use shall be made of radar equipment if fitted and operational, including long-range scanning to obtain early warning of risk of collision and radar plotting or equivalent systematic observation of detected objects.
(c) Assumptions shall not be made on the basis of scanty information, especially scanty radar information.
(d) In determining if risk of collision exists the following considerations shall be among those taken into account:
(i) such risk shall be deemed to exist if the compass bearing of an approaching vessel does not appreciably change;
(ii) such risk may sometimes exist even when an appreciable bearing change is evident, particularly when approaching a very large vessel or a tow or when approaching a vessel at close range.

Relative motion

We are used to the relative motion of other people, for example when we are moving around a busy public place like a town square. A person on foot realizes almost intuitively when someone else approaches via an unchanging direction and that this indicates a collision risk. But someone observing the same scene from a balcony can have a completely different impression of who is going to bump into whom. The correct interpretation of the radar screen poses a similar problem. We are on the balcony, without realising it!

The relative motion presented to us on the radar screen can be very useful when assessing the risk of collision – it just requires practice. Interpreting relative motion on the radar screen is not intuitive in the way that it is when walking around the town square, so it is a skill that you need to develop.

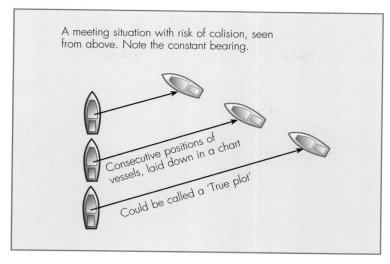

A meeting situation with risk of colision, seen from above. Note the constant bearing.

Consecutive positions of vessels, laid down in a chart

Could be called a 'True plot'

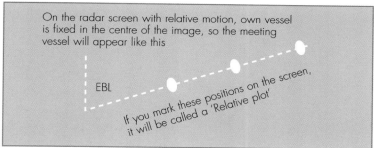

On the radar screen with relative motion, own vessel is fixed in the centre of the image, so the meeting vessel will appear like this

EBL

If you mark these positions on the screen, it will be called a 'Relative plot'

Using the EBL

A simple and reliable method for investigating the risk of collision is to place the EBL and VRM in conjunction over a contact. This will produce a cross on the screen over the present position of the contact. If the contact follows the EBL towards the centre of the screen, and you maintain your course, then there is a real risk of collision. If the contact remains under the cross it is a vessel with the same course and speed as you.

The contact in this picture has moved parallel to the Heading Mark from the EBL/VRM position. As long as it remains on this path there is no risk of collision.

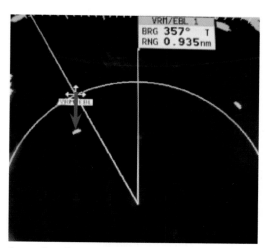

VRM/EBL 1
BRG 357° T
RNG 0.935nm

Remember that you can only monitor as many contacts as there are EBLs/VRMs available, which is usually two.

Using the Trail function

The Trail function is useful if you want to pinpoint moving contacts and keep an overall eye on the entire traffic situation. With this function activated, every contact gets a trail.

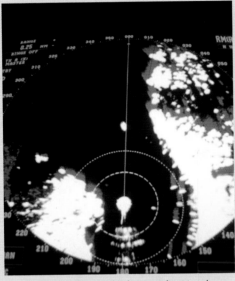

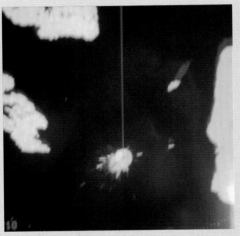

A contact with no trail, close to the Heading Mark. The target is a boat with the same speed and course as your vessel.

The trail of this contact shows that the contact (the 'blob' on the screen) is moving straight towards the centre of the screen. If it continues to do so, then sooner or later it will arrive at the centre, which is where we are. In other words, it suggests that there is a risk of collision.

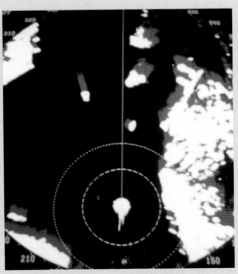

Four moving contacts and their trails. To port of the Heading Mark is a contact whose tail suggests that it is moving straight towards the centre of the screen, and therefore poses a risk of collision. The closest contact shows no sign of significant relative movement, so it must be a vessel whose course and speed is the same as our own. The two more distant contacts ahead are moving on different courses, crossing from right to left.

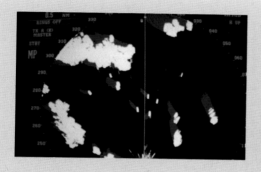

This picture shows a Head-up screen while our own vessel is altering course to port. The alteration of course makes it almost impossible to interpret the trails on the image.

The trail length is adjustable. They usually start to show on the screen after a few seconds and after a minute or so you are usually able to see which contacts are moving, and which of them may pose a risk of collision.

When your vessel is stationary and Trail is activated, all moving targets will generate trails in the direction of their course over ground, with a length in proportion to their speed over ground. Non-moving targets such as land and ships at anchor will have no trails.

The Trail function does not indicate a collision risk with great accuracy. The advantages of the method lie in its simplicity and its ability to give information all over the screen. You have to compensate for the lack of accuracy by making distinct manoeuvres in good time in order to avoid collision.

MARPA

MARPA (Mini-ARPA) is a semi-automatic tool that you can use to investigate the risk of collision. ARPA stands for Automatic Radar Plotting Aid, and is a function found in bigger radar sets.

The first step when using MARPA is to acquire a contact. You place the cursor over the relevant contact and press Acquire. The contact will now be marked with a square icon, and the radar will begin to track the target and compute its movements.

When sufficient data has been collected

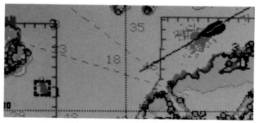

Here, the radar operator has placed the Cursor over the contact and pressed Acquire. A square icon marks the contact. The Radar overlay function is also in use with the radar image superimposed over the e-chart.

the square will change to display a circle and a vector will be marked on the screen, giving the heading and speed of target. You can then activate a 'box' which contains useful information about the target, amongst other things the CPA (Closest Point of Approach, i.e. minimum passing distance) and TCPA (Time to CPA). A MARPA list is also created, giving information on the different acquired targets.

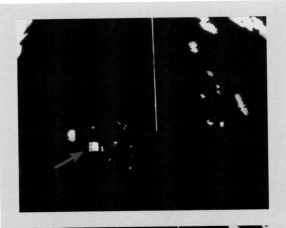

In this first screenshot the contact has been Acquired.

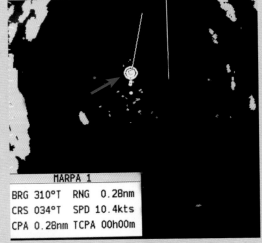

MARPA 1

BRG 310°T   RNG   0.28nm
CRS 034°T   SPD 10.4kts
CPA 0.28nm TCPA 00h00m

In this screenshot, the MARPA is displaying a circle and a vector, revealing the heading of the target. The dots behind the MARPA icon are old contact positions. The display box gives a lot of information about the target.

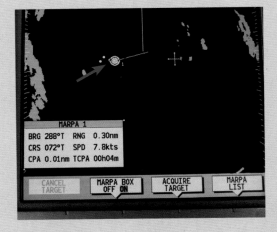

MARPA 1

BRG 288°T   RNG   0.30nm
CRS 072°T   SPD 7.8kts
CPA 0.01nm TCPA 00h04m

| CANCEL TARGET | MARPA BOX OFF ON | ACQUIRE TARGET | MARPA LIST |

In this third screenshot you can see that the target has altered course.

 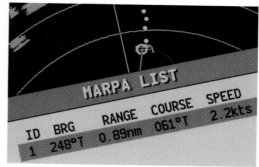

If the computed CPA is smaller than the safe value, the radar will sound an alarm.

The MARPA function should get speed and heading information from the log and the compass, not from GPS, in order to provide correct information for avoiding action.

Compared to the Trail function, MARPA has to be activated for every contact of interest. It is worth noting that in confined waters the situation may develop so rapidly that MARPA cannot always generate useful information.

Several factors reduce the accuracy of MARPA calculations:

- Quality of the vessel's speed and heading sensors, especially when at high speed.
- Bearing error caused by beam width distortion.
- When the other vessel is slow compared to yours.
- Where one or both vessels are changing heading and speed continuously.
- When the speed input is wrong the MARPA may give a false indication of the other vessel's heading (but information about CPA will still be correct).
- If the true contact vector (showing COG for target) is used when in the presence of currents it can give you a false impression of the situation. (The rules in the COLREGS don't refer to COG, but to Heading).

MARPA will stop tracking a target once it merges with another target. The same will happen when the contact is weak or intermittent. A lost target is signalled by an alarm.

Plotting

Plotting is a systematic way to register contacts and their movements. The first reason to plot is to determine the risk of collision and the second is to anticipate the avoiding action you will need to take. Plotting is calculating manually what the MARPA processor does automatically. The plot can be done on a special type of paper, known as a plotting sheet. Using a plotting sheet is unusual nowadays, but it is a very good exercise in understanding the problems that can arise from 'relative motion', as these should not be underestimated.

In principle, the plot can be done on the screen with a grease pencil or whiteboard marker, perhaps on a protective sheet stuck to the screen. Old radars had a special screen for this. On the open ocean the plotting period is usually six minutes on an unchanged course, as this is a tenth of an hour and makes calculations easy.

In confined waters there is seldom enough time for such a plot. A straight course is also an absolute condition for a plot when using Head-up mode, as an unsteady course will adversely affect the accuracy of the plot. Both the EBL method and the Trail function are able to highlight the risk of collision, but neither will tell you the course and speed of the other vessel. The plot does have that capability, providing you with a better basis for deciding your own avoiding action.

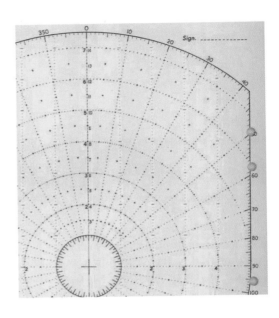

The plotting sheet, with its 'spider's web' of range rings and lines of bearings.

Radar-assisted collision

A classic situation is when two ships are crossing on nearly opposite courses, and ignorance of the course and speed of one ship has a crucial and sometimes fatal influence on the collision-avoiding manoeuvre of the other. One of the ships sees the contact of

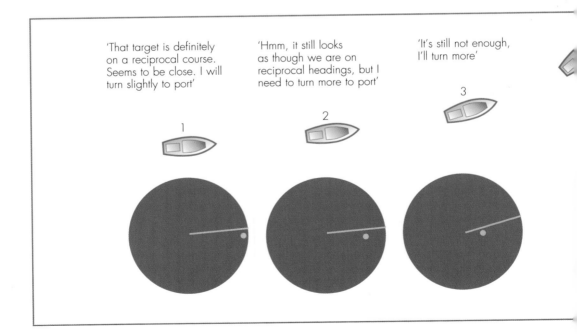

the other ship slightly to starboard of its Heading Mark, while the other ship sees the opposite contact slightly to port of its Heading Mark.

At this point they both make the same mistake. They assume – without evidence – that the other ship is actually on a parallel yet opposite course. In reality, their courses cross slightly, so they are both seriously wrong in believing that the situation is not developing into a possible collision. Instead, they both believe that the situation is developing fairly well, but each decides that the safe margin (CPA) is too small. The one with the contact to port of the Heading Mark thinks that a small adjustment to starboard is a good idea. The other, with the contact starboard of the Heading Mark, considers that a similar adjustment to port will improve the CPA. As the situation develops, neither of them is satisfied by the apparent CPA, so both continue their adjustments. They still believe in the idea of parallel courses!

It is not unusual for 'radar assisted collisions' to develop in this way. The result is a collision in which the ships hit each other at an angle of nearly 90 degrees. A very famous early case was the collision between *Stockholm* and *Andrea Doria* in 1956. In those days radar was a comparatively new instrument and officers had not been educated in the systematic plotting of contacts. However, this scenario has been repeated many times since, despite increasing awareness of the potential problem.

The origin of this type of collision stems from the fact that those in charge of the watch did not understand the course and speed of the other vessel. Investigations also reveal that moving too fast, insufficient look-out, numerous small course alterations, lack of fog signalling and the habit of accepting small safety margins has contributed to many accidents, and all these actions are contrary to the requirements of the Colregs. In some cases a defective radar or badly adjusted radar image is partly to blame.

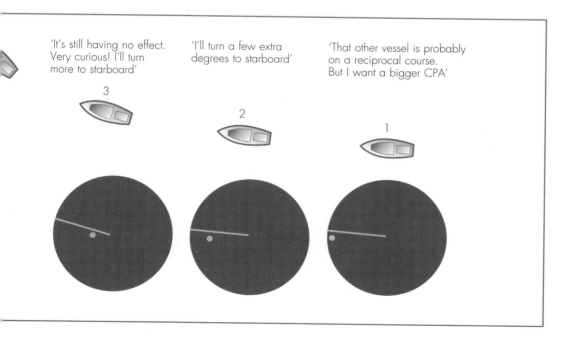

THE RELATIVE PLOT IN PRACTICE

Plotting in Head-up mode assumes that your own vessel maintains a constant course and speed. If these change you'll have to start a new plot. Even after an avoiding action, when your course causes the radar image to rotate, you need to start a new plot for the follow-up procedure.

If using the North-up mode, only the Heading Mark will move when the vessel is yawing and the radar image will not rotate when the vessel makes a course alteration.

- Note the contact's position (or record it using the bearing and range scales) and note the time.
- After 3 minutes, make a new mark.
- After 6 minutes, make one more mark.

A line drawn through the three marks will show the relative motion of the contact (relative trail). So far this information is the same as that given by Trail.

Continue drawing the line (or 'trail') through the marks and towards the centre of the screen. If neither vessel alters course or speed, the contact will approach your own vessel along the prolonged trail.

Even this very simple plot is enough to provide several important pieces of information:

1. The shortest distance between the extended trail and the centre of the screen represents the Closest Point of Approach.
2. If you have plotted at regular intervals, you can estimate the time at which the approaching vessel will reach its CPA (called the TCPA) by projecting the 3 minute step forward along the prolonged trail (which may be called the projected, extended or predicted trail).

3. If the prolonged trail crosses the Heading Mark, it means the other vessel is going to pass ahead of you, and you will pass astern of it.

When the CPA is sufficiently large (that is, outside the safety margin) all you have to do is to follow up the contact and ensure that it follows the prolonged trail.

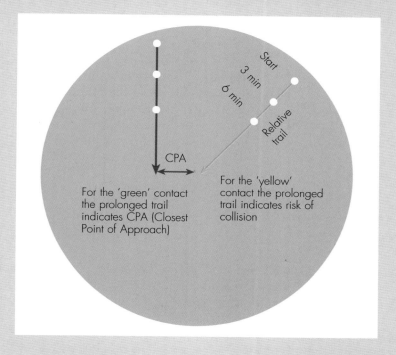

Start

3 min

6 min

Relative trail

CPA

For the 'green' contact the prolonged trail indicates CPA (Closest Point of Approach)

For the 'yellow' contact the prolonged trail indicates risk of collision

10 Taking avoiding action in the open sea

When the plot or your observations indicate a risk of collision, you MUST take avoiding action. The rules demand that:

> **Rule 8 (a)** Any action taken to avoid collision shall be taken in accordance with the Rules of this Part and shall, if the circumstances of the case admit, be positive, made in ample time and with due regard to the observance of good seamanship.
>
> **Rule 19(d)** A vessel which detects by radar alone the presence of another vessel shall determine if a close-quarters situation is developing and/or risk of collision exists. If so, she shall take avoiding action in ample time...

Altering course

In general you should always avoid altering course to port except when overtaking (when you have the option), or when a faster vessel is approaching from your starboard quarter. In that situation it is obviously unwise to turn so as to cross the predicted track of an overtaking vessel, so the Rule encourages you to turn to port, away from the approaching vessel.

The Colregs set out principles and give some detailed instructions concerning the behaviour of vessels in restricted visibility, but there is still much that is left to the initiative and decision of the person in charge of the vessel. For example, 'in ample time' should as a minimum be considered to mean 'in time to avoid a collision'. But 'restricted visibility' is not defined, neither is 'substantial', 'good seamanship' or 'close-quarters situation'. They all have to be interpreted in relation to the vessels involved, in the prevailing situation.

According to Rule 19 both vessels involved are required to take avoiding action. The question isn't 'Who has who on the starboard side?' or 'Who is overtaking?' (as it is when in sight of one another). When such action consists of an alteration of course, the following shall be **avoided**, as far as possible:

> **Rule 19d (i)** an alteration of course to port for a vessel forward of the beam, other than for a vessel being overtaken;
> (ii) an alteration of course towards a vessel abeam or abaft the beam.

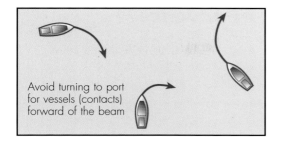

An alteration of course is the most common and often the most effective avoiding action to be taken in the open sea.

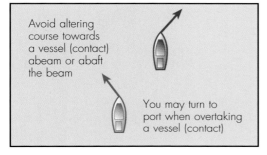

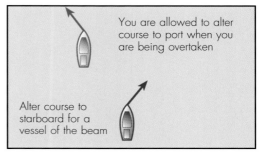

Rule 19 is sometimes regarded as primarily written for big ships on the open sea, but it applies to everyone. Investigations of cases, mostly from accidents involving big ships on the open sea, have highlighted difficulties, different interpretations, or even an unwillingness to comply with Rule 19. For example, stress resulting from too tight a schedule may lead a watchkeeper to compromise the safe application of the rules.

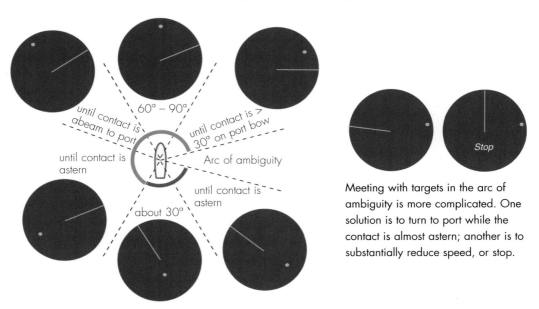

Meeting with targets in the arc of ambiguity is more complicated. One solution is to turn to port while the contact is almost astern; another is to substantially reduce speed, or stop.

Recommended avoiding actions when altering course, according to Rule 19. Contact in green sector – turn to starboard. Contact in red sector – turn to port. (Radar images show situation after avoiding action.)

Planning avoiding actions in advance

In open water the radar plot is the best way to understand the movement of other vessels and how to take effective evasive action, but in confined waters, such as rivers, it is not much use as there is rarely enough time to make the plot.

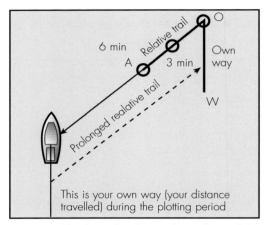
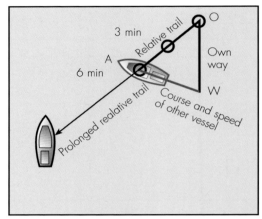

A situation like this will end up with a collision if the vessels involved fail to take avoiding action, because the 'relative trail' shows that the contact is moving straight towards the centre of the screen.

Draw a line from the first mark in the plot parallel to the Heading Mark, to represent the track of your ship during 6 minutes (one tenth of an hour). For example, if your speed is 10 knots, that line has to represent 1 mile. This represents the direction and distance that the contact would move on the screen if the contact was stationary, and just drifting with the tide.

Many radar observers like to label the original position of the contact with the letter 'O' (for 'Original') and label the other end of the line with the letter 'W' so that the line 'WO' represents the 'Way of Own' vessel.

At the same time, they label the actual position of the contact with the letter 'A' (for 'Approaching'), so that the line 'OA' represents the 'Observed or Apparent' movement of the contact.

Finally, the line WA represents the difference between where the other vessel would have been if she was stationary, and where she really is. In other words, it is the change in position caused by her own movement. Rather conveniently the letters serve as a reminder that the line WA represents the Way of the Approaching vessel (the red line in the diagram above right).

The information in the triangle enables you to work out an appropriate avoiding action.

If the positions W and A were plotted six minutes after the initial plot at O, then the length of the line WA represents the distance the other vessel has travelled through the water in six minutes. Six minutes is one tenth of an hour, so the other vessel's speed in knots is ten times the length of the line WA.

The direction of the line WA represents the direction the other vessel is steering, relative to our own heading.

Before discussing more sophisticated types of evasive action, let us first look at the most basic ways to avoid collision. First, stopping completely (see below left) and second, changing course to travel parallel with, but in the opposite direction to, that of the other vessel (see below right).

These actions will both result in the same CPA, but this will be accomplished more quickly by altering course. Furthermore as the plot has rotated (when Head-up) you will have to start a new plot for the follow-up procedure. For these reasons it is often a better choice to stop when in confined waters.

If time and space allow, then evasive action doesn't have to be so dramatic. You have to decide on an adequate safety margin (ie your minimum CPA, which must be suitable for the vessel and the area in which you are operating).

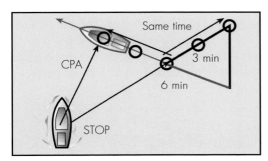
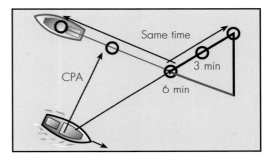

Reducing speed

Mark off your minimum CPA (safety margin) around own vessel (red circle). Draw a tangent to the perimeter through the 6 minute mark. This is the line that you want the contact to follow.

To calculate the necessary speed reduction (to avoid a collision by your own efforts only) you prolong the line marked 'Desired trail of contact' to cut the line O-W. Your required speed is then described by the vector 'New speed' (= your movement during one tenth of an hour). A speed reduction means that you keep to the intended track. By reducing speed you do not create new dramatic situations with other vessels and the reduced speed gives you more time to consider the situation. (However, new situations may occur as vessels overtake.)

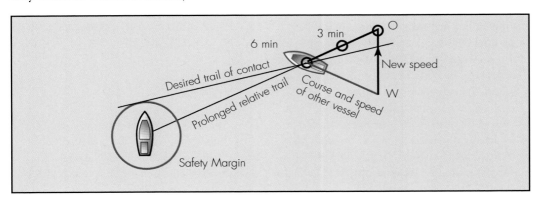

Changing course

You calculate an avoiding action by altered course in the following way: Lay off the distance 'own way' (O-W) with dividers. Place one of the points on W and with the other point intersect the extension of the 'Desired trail of contact'. Join the point of intersection to W. The angle described between your own way (O-W) and the new line gives the required angle for your alteration of course.

The accuracy of the plot in Head-up mode is mainly dependant on the helmsman's ability to keep a straight course. Yawing about during plotting can produce significant errors, which can ruin your correct assessment of the situation. Bad course keeping ability, resulting in a less reliable plot, has to be compensated for by increasing the safety margin.

Another source of error, which can take some time to discover, occurs if the other vessel alters its course or speed (see further information on page 81). Your observations and calculations become redundant as fast as they are completed! Taking evasive action by an alteration of course will also make the image on the radar screen rotate if you are using the Head-up mode. Therefore, when the alteration is complete you should start a new plot in order to assess the outcome of the change. In North-up mode only the Heading marker will move as the vessel rotates.

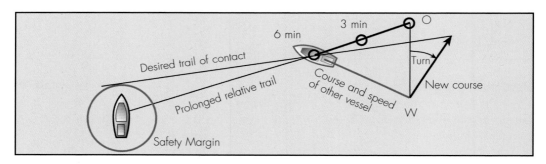

Rules 7(c) and (d)
(c) Assumptions shall not be made on the basis of scanty information, especially scanty radar information.
(d) In determining if risk of collision exists the following considerations shall be among those taken into account:
(i) such risk shall be deemed to exist if the compass bearing of an approaching vessel does not appreciably change;
(ii) such risk may sometimes exist even when an appreciable bearing change is evident, particularly when approaching a very large vessel or a tow or when approaching a vessel at close range.

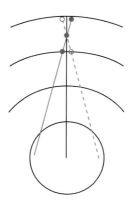

A small plotting error can cause a significant error in the predicted trail. Because the Trail function works continuously, an unsteady course will be obvious immediately.

Avoiding actions in practice

Let us now look at some examples. In these cases collision is avoided by the vessel's own manoeuvre only. In fact you don't even know if the other vessel has radar. If the other vessel takes avoiding action, you should detect it during your follow-up procedure and you might be able to return to your previous course fairly soon.

The figure below demonstrates the problem of interpreting Trails during one minute (one at a time, not all together!). The safety margin is 0.25 miles on the basis of your vessel's manoeuvrability, quality of radar observations, crew, weather conditions and shipping lane traffic. We assume the speed of your vessel is 10 knots.

Trail 1 shows a target approaching on the port bow with the same speed as your own vessel. An alteration of your course by 45 degrees to starboard will result in a meeting outside the safety margin area. Instead of changing course, you could reduce speed to 3 knots, in which case the other vessel would pass ahead of you.

Trail 2 shows a target on a counter-course to your own vessel, and with the same speed. In this situation you might be tempted to alter course to port in order to increase the passing distance (CPA). On no account do this, because the other vessel may be thinking of turning to starboard! If you turn to port, you will simply confuse the other vessel. If you alter course 55 degrees to starboard the meeting will be outside your safety margin. Stopping your vessel in this case won't actually increase the CPA.

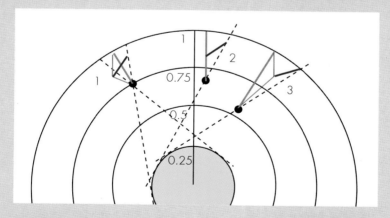

- Grey lines are the trails.
- Thin green lines are your own way.
- The red lines are the way of the other ship.
- The thick blue lines are your new course to avoid collision by the alteration of your own course only.

In congested waters it is a wise precaution to lay your intended track on the starboard side of a traffic lane. This will decrease the likelihood of a critical situation developing. If this kind of situation is to be resolved in sight of each other it's essential to proceed at low speed until visual contact, so that the vessels involved have time to analyse their counterpart's course and speed before taking further action.

Trail 3 shows a vessel making 20 knots on a course that will cross your track. Your course alteration to starboard must be no less than 75 degrees. The alternative is to slow down, but even if your vessel is stopped the meeting will still take place within the safety area. This example clearly shows that the speed of the faster vessel has a dominating influence on how the situation will develop.

We shall now look at an example of a contact in the sector of ambiguity, under conditions of poor visibility. You detect a contact to starboard and slightly forward of the beam and consider that a risk of collision exists. You plot the contact over the next 6 minutes, with your own vessel making 10 knots. The plot shows that the other vessel's course is crossing yours by 25 degrees, its speed is slightly higher than yours and there is a risk of collision. During the previous 6 minutes the distance between you has closed by 0.5 miles, which now leaves you with 18 minutes until collision.

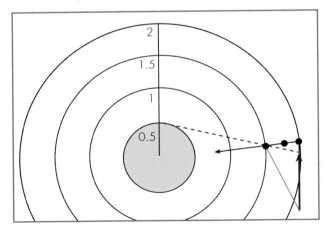

Plotting the contact.

Both vessels have the other forward of the beam. Both have to take action to avoid collision according to Rule 19. According to this the other vessel is supposed to alter course to starboard. Under the same rule you are also permitted to veer to starboard. Both of you have the option of reducing your speed. According to the plot, a speed reduction on your part (blue arrow = 8 knots) will result in the specified safety margin.

However, this is a minor speed reduction and will not easily be detected by the other vessel. Start by substantially reducing your speed by about 5 knots. This makes your action much clearer to the other vessel and reduces the likelihood of confusion.

By reducing your speed, navigation is made easier and there is more time to follow up any developments. Manoeuvres made in sight of each other can be carried out with greater security.

However, do be aware that if the other vessel also slows down as much as you do, the risk of collision is still present!

What about avoiding collision by altering course (see diagram below)? If a collision has to be avoided by your own manoeuvre only, a turn of 50 degrees to starboard is needed according to the plot (assuming the turn is started at the 6 minute mark). Of course your radar image will turn by the same extent. A new plot is needed for following up (see triangle of dashed lines).

The alteration of course creates a new situation with new navigational requirements and new risks of collision with other vessels in the vicinity. Turning towards another vessel also increases the relative speed of approach.

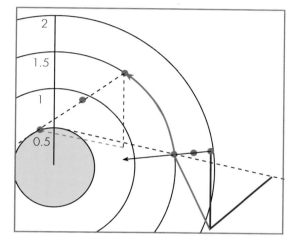

Avoiding collision by altering course.

The same situation is shown on what is called a 'true plot' (see diagram below). Each side of the square is 2 miles long. The arrows show the movement of the two vessels during the 6 minutes after your 50 degrees course alteration. Your vessel will have to travel about 0.8 miles from her intended track before being able to resume her proper course, provided that the second vessel changes neither heading nor speed.

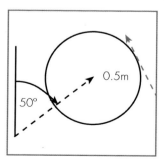

A true plot.

11 | Close-quarters situations

Rule 19 does not define a 'close-quarters' situation in metres and other sources are not very helpful. (According to Cahill, in *Collisions and Their Causes*, you should be able to avoid a collision by unilateral manoeuvres only, despite the behaviour of the other vessel).

Rule 19(d) is unambiguous about (but not limited to) situations on the open sea (see page 70). Avoiding action shall be undertaken in ample time, often by an alteration of course. For close quarters situations Rule 19(e) states:

Rule 19 (e) Except where it has been determined that a risk of collision does not exist, every vessel which hears apparently forward of her beam the fog signal of another vessel, or which cannot avoid a close-quarters situation with another vessel forward of her beam, shall reduce her speed to the minimum at which she can be kept on her course. She shall if necessary take all her way off and in any event navigate with extreme caution until danger of collision is over.

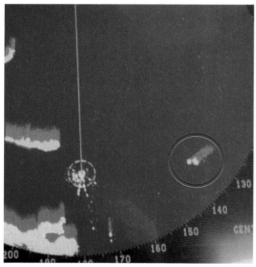

Although there is a target to starboard, the Trail function shows that there is no risk of collision at the moment. But keep observing the screen.

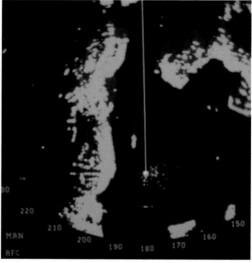

When ships meet each other, each on the correct side of a fairway, it is usually assumed that there is no risk of collision.

This rule deals with two situations in which you are obliged either to reduce your speed to the slowest possible, but still keep your course, or stop altogether:

- When a fog signal has been heard, apparently forward of the beam.
- When you cannot avoid a close-quarters situation with another ship, also forward of the beam – for example when there is no room for a sufficient alteration of course.

However, there is one exception to the slowing down rule, and this is when no risk of collision is verified (for example, by reliable radar observations). In this case a VHF call is a useful way to discuss how a situation can be handled. However, such discussions have in themselves given rise to misunderstanding. Recommendations vary between countries – the UK's MCA discourages the use of VHF in collision avoidance.

Avoiding action in restricted visibility and in confined waters

In such a situation you need to ask 'Which action is the safest?' Aim for a bigger CPA, altering your course according to Rule 19(d).

This will move your vessel closer to the navigational hazards. It will also create new situations in relation to other vessels in the vicinity. You'll need to monitor your contacts, and consider any new navigational requirements. You also need to take account of Rule 6 'Safe speed', and Rule 9 'Narrow channels', which require you to keep to the starboard side of the fairway.

If you believe that slowing down and awaiting a meeting in a close-quarters situation, maybe within sight of each other, is a better avoiding action than altering course, you have to decide if it is in accordance with Rule 2(b):

Rule 2 (b) In construing and applying these Rules due regard shall be had to all dangers of navigation and collision and to all special circumstances, including the limitations of the vessels involved, which may make a departure from these Rules necessary to avoid immediate danger.

Is it necessary to depart from Rule 19, to avoid immediate danger? This is a demanding situation in which you have to:

- Maintain a safe speed.
- Keep a sharp look-out.
- Continue to observe your contacts systematically.
- Sound your fog signal.
- Keep to the starboard side of the fairway.
- Keep a close watch on your own heading and position.

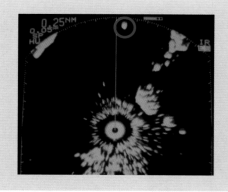

A contact suddenly appears at 0.25 miles. With the radar set to such an extremely short range, there is no option but to reduce speed immediately. You can't turn to starboard in such confined waters and you must not even consider turning to port. Maintain your course with reduced speed, keep a good look-out and sound the fog signal.

It is essential that you make your own assessment of what a 'safe speed' is . The old concept of 'moderate speed' requires that a vessel is able to stop within half the limit of visibility. This is still considered to be a good working definition of 'safe speed' for small craft in confined waters.

A rapid visual detection is essential. Even a few seconds' delay in sighting another vessel reduces your safety margin considerably. You need a safety margin both for your own delay (your thinking time) and for unexpected manoeuvres by approaching ships. Do also remember that visibility may suddenly deteriorate, without your noticing.

For example, if two vessels meet in confined waters, each one making 10 knots, they are approaching each other at 20 knots, or 10 metres per second. When you are looking at the 1/4 mile Range on the screen, you have 463 metres to the edge of the screen, where new contacts appear. The collision point is halfway between. That leaves you with 46 seconds to collision if neither vessel does anything!

It is also important not to have pre-conceived ideas about the approaching vessel. She may be constrained by her depth, have no radar, or a defective or poorly adjusted one! Remember also that in restricted visibility there is no such thing as 'Right of Way'.

You should regard all vessels in close proximity as potential hazards, and don't

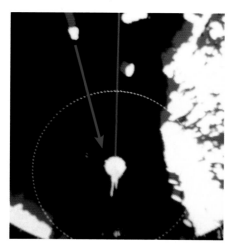

become accustomed to close meetings at too high a speed! Remember that you don't know your counterpart's opinion on the situation, or how he/she is going to react. And remember that the radar set has to be adjusted to deliver the information you need.

Here the VRM is placed at 0.2 M. It is placed there as a reminder of what is considered to be a close-quarters situation for this vessel, in this traffic situation. The Trail function indicates a risk of collision with the Contact on the port bow. Our vessel is positioned to starboard in the traffic lane – a simple precaution!

Follow-up

While undertaking an avoiding action in clear weather, you will soon see if your action has been effective and if the other vessel is going to do anything – helpful or not! Of course, in restricted visibility this is all very different. Unlike a visual look-out, the relative movement of the contact on the radar screen won't show at a glance what the other vessel is doing.

Having taken avoiding action you are faced with three new problems: 'Has my manoeuvre been big enough?'; 'Has the other vessel noticed my manoeuvre?'; 'Will the other vessel carry out a manoeuvre?'. The diagram below shows how a course alteration by the approaching vessels may appear on your screen and how the relative trails are affected.

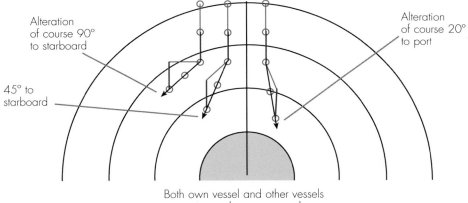

Alteration of course 90° to starboard

Alteration of course 20° to port

45° to starboard

Both own vessel and other vessels are going at the same speed

Your vessel and the approaching vessels are on opposite courses, at the same speed. During one time period all vessels are steering straight courses. In the next period the approaching vessels are turning 20 degrees, 45 degrees and 90 degrees respectively. The black arrows in the figure show how their relative trails are affected. From this we can easily see that a course alteration of 20 degrees may not be easy to detect by another vessel.

A problem when using relative presentation is that actions by other vessels are not easily detected. However, as your speed reduces, the movements on the radar screen are a more accurate reflection of the situation on the water.

The diagram on page 82 shows what happens on the screen when two oncoming vessels alter their courses by 45 degrees. One of them is twice as fast as your vessel. The other is making half the speed of your vessel. If your vessel hasn't altered course, the trails will look like this. To work out a course alteration by an approaching vessel when you have also made a turn is even more difficult, as the radar images will turn (when in Head-up mode). When using North-up the radar image is stable but still relative. In True motion mode you will see the course alterations made by other vessels, but the risk of collision is not so easy to work out.

The most important requirement when following up an avoiding action is to keep other vessels out of your safety area. If necessary, achieve this by reducing your speed or even stopping completely, and if the visibility is poor sound fog signals more frequently. And remember – the fog may become thicker without your noticing!

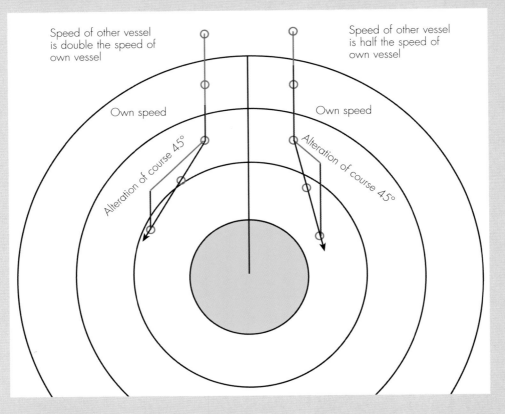

In visual contact

The last phase of a meeting situation in confined waters may be so close that the vessels come within sight of each other. The situation is then governed by the 'usual' rules concerning crossing courses, meeting head on, overtaking and so forth. Now, but not earlier, you can leave Rule 19 and you are permitted to sound manoeuvre signals.

Meetings in sight of each other in foggy weather presume, until that moment, that fog signals are sounded, navigation lights are lit, a proper lookout is kept and that the speed is slow (the reduction depending on the manoeuvrability of the ship).

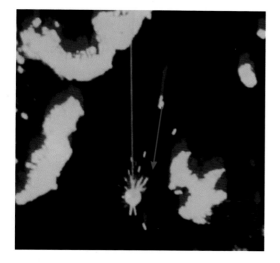

In this screenshot, there is a contact from an oncoming vessel to starboard of our heading line. The trail of the contact is indicating a risk of collision, or at least a close-quarters situation. You cannot alter course to starboard towards the track of the oncoming vessel. Although the extra sea room is tempting, you can't turn to port in case the approaching vessel turns to starboard. You have to meet within visual contact and at low speed.

When you make visual contact with a boat in fog, Rule 19 no longer applies.

12 | The human element

The radar set is a demanding instrument, and you need to adjust it to find the information you need. Training is invaluable, and you must remain alert, especially in confined waters. It is all too easy to have too short a range in that situation, which makes it more difficult to detect other vessels. Gain and Sea Clutter are also difficult to adjust correctly.

When a collision occurs in fog, the person in charge is invariably criticized. The investigations point out over and over again that the look-out and follow up of contacts were insufficient. On the water you have to make your own judgement of what 'in ample time', 'substantial action', 'safe speed', 'safe distance', 'systematically observe' and 'close quarters situation' mean, so that you can transform the intentions set out in the rules into positive action.

It is very easy to make assumptions regarding the likely behaviour of approaching vessels, for example 'they must be following the traffic lane', 'they are probably keeping to the starboard side of the fairway'. You don't really know what another vessel is doing in confined waters until you have observed them for at least half a minute on the radar screen – while maintaining a steady course yourself.

Many investigations also point out that the rules for vessels in sight of each other have incorrectly influenced their behaviour in fog. A vessel discovered on the port side has been considered to be a 'give away vessel' and the observer's as the 'stand on vessel' – completely wrong. Rule 19 contains the obvious intention that vessels should avoid close quarters situations in the first place. Your avoiding action has to be taken in ample time and to be sufficiently large to be detectable by other vessels. The rules require a lot of decisions from the person in charge, and the possibility of human error remains. Historically there are many, many cases in which human errors resulted in a collision. Don't contribute to that list!

A meeting situation in fog develops in several phases:

1 Discovering a new target on the radar screen.
2 Evaluating the risk of collision.
3 Deciding which rules govern the situation.
4 Acting according to the rules.
5 Following up to see if the action taken is sufficient. If not, taking further action.

You can make an error of judgement or a mistake at every single step of this chain!

We shall now examine two cases, both investigated by the MAIB (Marine Accident Investigating Branch), that each have a good deal to tell us about human behaviour. The intention behind the investigations is to find out what really happened, rather than allocate blame, and to publicise the lessons learned to prevent further accidents. An accident is seldom dependent on a single fault: more often it is the result of a chain of errors.

Wahkuna and *P&O Nedlloyd Vespucci*

Wahkuna was a Moody 47 on a cross-Channel passage in poor visibility on a heading of 012 degrees and motoring at a speed of 7.5 knots. She was sounding fog signals and carrying a crew of five, skippered by her owner. *P&O NV* was a container ship of 66,000 tonnes, bound from Antwerp to Singapore, on a heading of 255 degrees, at a speed of 25 knots (which could hardly be considered to be safe given the circumstances). She was manned by three people on the bridge: Master, Officer of the Watch and a look-out. The visibility was 50 metres.

P&O Nedlloyd Vespucci.

Wahkuna after the collision.

Discovery of the target on the radar
Wahkuna detected the contact of *P&O NV* at a range of 6 miles.

P&O NV detected the contact of *Wahkuna* at a range of between 5–6 miles on the port bow.

Evaluating the risk of collision
The skipper of *Wahkuna* estimated by eye from his radar that the target would pass ahead at a distance of 1.6 miles. He continued to track the radar target visually until the range had decreased to 3 miles, by which time he assumed the vessels were on a collision course.

On *P&O NV*, according to ARPA, the contact would pass 0.8 miles ahead.

Action to avoid collision
The skipper of *Wahkuna* disengaged the engine and slowed down.

On *P&O NV* the loss of speed by *Wahkuna* worried the master. At this time the contact of *Wahkuna* was on the port bow at a range of between 1.5–2 miles. Now the CPA seemed to be only 0.2 miles to port. In spite of this, *P&O NV* altered neither course nor speed. The master accepted a safety margin that was too small.

Wahkuna's action was based on scanty information, contravening Rule 7(c) of the Colregs. As the vessels finally collided without *P&O NV* altering either course or speed, it is evident that had the yacht not reduced her speed, she would have passed safely ahead of the container ship.

Follow-up

Aboard *Wahkuna*, after making the assessment that the container ship would pass ahead, no radar watch was maintained. Had it been, it would have been evident that the container ship was closing rapidly and further avoiding action could have been taken. *Wahkuna* lost steerage and didn't keep her course, in fact she turned to starboard, then turned slightly back and was hit by *NV* on her port bow.

MAIB findings

The investigation found that on *P&O NV* they were over-confident in the accuracy of their ARPA plot. The speed input was not taken from the ship's log, which is a requirement for anti-collision evaluation. Some minutes later the collision occurred, without being noticed by anyone onboard *P&O NV*. The subsequent investigation found that several factors had contributed to the accident, including:

1 Misunderstanding by *Wahkuna*'s skipper as to which of the Colregs were applicable in fog.
2 Over-confidence in the accuracy of ARPA by the Master of *P&O NV*.
3 Acceptance by the master of *P&O NV* of a small passing distance.
4 The inability of the yacht skipper to use radar effectively.
5 The failure of both vessels to keep an effective radar look-out.
6 The high speed of *P&O NV*.
7 Poor bridge resource management.

For the full report go to: http://www.maib.gov.uk/cms_resources/nedlloyd%20 vespucci%20and%20wahkuna.pdf

Whispa and *Gas Monarch*

The collision between *Whispa* and *Gas Monarch* took place 6 miles from Lowestoft on 16 April 2007 in dense fog, with visibility being at between 50m and 150m. *Whispa* was motoring on her auxiliary engine at 4.5 knots, proceeding northwards. *Gas Monarch* was making a good 14.3 knots, on a southerly heading. There was a south-going tidal stream of 2 knots. No fog signals were sounded by either vessel. *Whispa* had her skipper on watch, and *Gas Monarch* was manned by her 3rd officer and a look-out.

Discovery of the target on the radar

Whispa detected the contact of *Gas Monarch* at 6 miles on the port bow. *Gas Monarch* detected the contact of *Whispa* ahead at just over 6 miles.

Whispa.

Gas Monarch.

Evaluating the risk of collision

Whispa monitored, but didn't plot, the track of the target close to the Heading Mark for several miles. At a range of less than 3 miles the skipper believed that the vessels were on a collision course. Had *Whispa's* skipper plotted *Gas Monarch* effectively, he would have found out that, although a close-quarters situation was developing, the two vessels were actually not on a collision course.

Gas Monarch calculated that the contact would pass clear to starboard. In making this decision, the 3rd officer used an EBL, VRM and trails of the contact, but no ARPA. The 3rd officer's observations of *Whispa* were not systematic, as required by Colregs Rule 7(b), and the method of calculating the CPA was unreliable. After losing radar contact, the 3rd officer assumed that *Whispa* would pass clear on his starboard side, so there was no reason for *Gas Monarch* to alter course.

Action to avoid collision

At a range of 3 miles, *Whispa* altered course 50 degrees to starboard. This action brought the two vessels onto a collision path.

Aboard *Gas Monarch*, and with the contact at 5.5 miles, the 3rd officer altered course 5 degrees to port in an attempt to create a starboard-to-starboard passing situation. He estimated the CPA to be 1 mile on the starboard side.

Follow-up

After the course alteration of 50 degrees the skipper of *Whispa* found that instead of tracking clear down his port side as expected, the contact appeared still to be coming towards him, now from a relative bearing of 50 degrees from the port bow. As the vessels closed *Whispa's* skipper altered a further 20 degrees to starboard, but still the contact continued to close on a steady bearing.

Aboard *Gas Monarch*, and at a range of 3 miles, the trail of *Whispa's* contact indicated a reduced CPA of 0.7 miles. Soon after this the contact was lost on the screen.

Technical errors

When the contact of *Whispa* was lost from both radars, the 3rd officer attempted to retune them by altering the Range scales and adjusting the Sea and Rain Clutter controls. On completion of adjustments, the radars were on Auto Tune, with Sea Anti-clutter set manually at about 1/3 sensitivity, while the Rain Anti-clutter was set at maximum suppression; these settings would have effectively masked weak images. Further confirmation of this is that, when on the 1.5-mile range scale, the radar screen was clear with no speckles on it; an obvious sign of over-suppression. The combination of poor radar tuning due to operator inexperience, and magnetron (transmitter) deterioration, may explain the loss of the contact from both radars.

The heading marker on *Whispa*'s radar was later found to have a starboard error of no less than 2 degrees. Because of this the radar target of *Gas Monarch* was displayed on the radar screen slightly to port of her real bearing relative to *Whispa*. The presence of the equipment encouraged *Whispa*'s skipper to attempt to navigate by radar without having enough knowledge and understanding of the equipment's functionality to do so safely, and while being unaware of the heading marker error.

MAIB findings

The MAIB investigation identified a number of contributing factors to the accident, including:

1 A failure by both vessels to abide by collision avoidance regulations.
2 Deteriorated performance and accuracy of both vessels' radars.
3 Lack of experience by the 3rd officer of *Gas Monarch*, compounded by lack of support from the Master.
4 Inappropriate use of radar equipment by both vessels.

For the full report go to: http://www.maib.gov.uk/cms_resources/Whispa_Gas%20 Monarch-published.pdf

13 | Seeing and being seen

Radar reflectors

It is essential to be seen by other vessels and a radar reflector is often represented as being a simple way to improve your visibility. Reflectors come in a variety of designs and are generally classified into three groups: octohedral, stacked arrays and lenses, but it is important to be aware that none of them guarantees that you will be seen by other vessels. The MAIB report into the loss of the *Ouzo* included a comprehensive review of the radar reflectors available to small craft, and found that none of them met current performance standards.

Octohedrals are made from plates of reflective material, such as aluminium alloy, mounted perpendicular to each other. When a radar pulse strikes the reflector, it will be bounced back in the same direction, regardless of the angle of incidence An octahedral is generally cheap, light and simple. For optimum performance, it should be mounted in what is often called the 'catch-rain' position – the position that it would naturally assume if it was lying on a horizontal surface.

Stacked array reflectors are usually enclosed within a cylindrical plastic casing, but inside they are built like a stack of octohedrals, using metal plates to form a number of corners which reflect the radar pulses.

Lens reflectors consist of a plastic sphere, which refracts radar energy onto a reflecting material. The reflected energy then passes back through the lens which concentrates it into a beam, returning the same way it came.

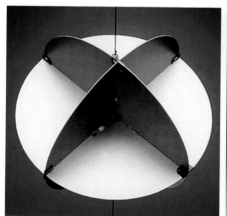
Octohedral reflector, in 'catch-rain' position.

Stacked array reflector.

Tri-lens reflector.

Radar cross section

The performance of radar reflectors is usually measured in terms of their radar cross section (RCS) or Equivalent Echoing Area (EEA), expressed in square metres.

The radar cross section of a radar reflector is usually considerably bigger than the physical size of the reflector suggests. A piece of flat steel, the size of an A4 sheet of paper, for instance, can have a radar section of about 48 square metres. This is because the measurement compares the radar response of the reflector with that of a smooth metal sphere whose cross section is 1 square metre.

A sphere is chosen as the reference because it produces an absolutely consistent response, regardless of the direction from which the radar waves approach it or the wavelength or frequency of the waves concerned. Unfortunately, a sphere is a very poor reflector.

Unlike a sphere, however, the performance of a flat plate is highly directional: if it is tilted or twisted even a few degrees out of its optimum position, it reflects nothing back to the radar but scatters all the energy away in the wrong direction. Any practical radar reflector is an attempt to combine the reflective efficiency of a flat metal plate with the all-round consistency of a sphere. This is almost never completely successful, so the performance of a radar reflector is usually affected by the angle at which the radar waves strike it. Because of this, the performance of a radar reflector is often presented in the form of a graph known as a polar diagram.

Radar transponders

Radar transponders differ from radar reflectors in that they respond to a radar pulse by transmitting a distinctive return signal of their own.

Racons are fitted on navigation marks, so that they can easily be distinguished from other contacts. The racon signal is a series of dots and dashes indicating a letter of the Morse code on the radar screen. The signal will come and go on your screen, because the racon transmits on several frequencies in sequence. Note that broadband radars don't receive Racon signals.

SART.

Radar target enhancer.

SARTs (Search And Rescue Transponders) are intended for use aboard liferafts to indicate their position. They produce a radially oriented line of 12 dots on the radar screen.

Radar target enhancers (RTEs) can be used instead of passive reflectors. The concept is similar to a racon, except that an RTE produces a very short pulse that mimics the appearance of an ordinary contact, but stronger and more consistent. If you choose to use a passive reflector as well as an RTE, it is important to make sure that the passive reflector is mounted well above or below the RTE, to minimize the risk of the RTE transmissions being reflected straight back to it from the reflector.

The **Automatic Identification System** (AIS) is a transponder system which is compulsory for most commercial vessels. A transponder on the ship transmits its name, MMSI (Maritime Mobile Service Identity) and type of ship, COG, SOG etc. The data is sent by VHF to other vessels in the vicinity, and the result will normally be presented on an e-chart or a radar screen. The primary idea of AIS is to detect vessels that are in radar shadow behind high islands or hidden by heavy sea clutter. As the course, speed and position data is coming directly from the vessel's own sensors, it is possible to detect an alteration in course or speed by other vessels more quickly, and as the MMSI is included in the information it is possible to call up the other ship directly by VHF, reducing the risk of misunderstanding.

There are three types of AIS equipment available:

AIS Type A is a high specification device, intended primarily for commercial vessels.

AIS Type B is a cheaper device intended for vessels which are not required by law to carry AIS, but whose owners choose to fit it. It is fully compatible with Class A equipment on other vessels, but transmits less information, at lower power and lower frequently.

Receive-Only AIS is also available. The cheapest of the three, it allows AIS details from other ships to be displayed on a chartplotter or radar screen, but does not inform other vessels of its presence.

Never assume that the radar reflector is a guarantee that you will be seen on the radar screen of another vessel. Not even AIS can guarantee that. But carrying radar and displaying a reflector are sensible, seamanlike actions and may one day save your life at sea. In thick fog they are the only aids that will help you to avoid collision.

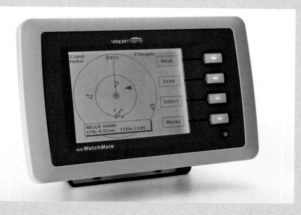

The screen on a receive-only AIS, with symbols of surrounding ships.

Glossary

AFC The electronic circuit that controls the autotune function.

AIS (Automatic Identification System) A system which sends actual data about vessels which can be seen on an electronic chart system, a radar screen or on a stand-alone display.

Antenna The revolving radar antenna can be open or covered by a radome.

Anti-clutter Electronic functions for removing the effect of annoying contacts. It is effective over the entire radar screen while AC Sea is effective to a limited range of a few miles.

ARPA (Automatic Radar Plotting Aid) A computerized function on big radars that enables them to track automatically and to analyze data for contacts on the screen in order to investigate risk of collision.

Beam width The width (in degrees) of the sector in which most of the radar's energy is transmitted. It is horizontally ca 1 degree on big radars and up to ca 6 degrees on small craft radars. Vertical beam width is about 25 – 30 degrees.

Blind sector A sector in which the radar cannot detect any targets because an obstruction on the vessel blocks the signal.

Brilliance A radar adjustment that controls the general brightness of the screen.

Broadband radar A new technology using extremely long pulses at very low power and constantly varying frequency.

Clutter Unwanted contacts from waves, rain or snow (see Anti-clutter).

COG Course over ground. The actual direction a vessel is moving over the ground. Also known as Ground Track.

Colregs International Regulations for Preventing Collisions at Sea.

Contact A blob on the radar screen, created by the reflected energy returning from a target.

Course-up A stabilized presentation mode in which the Heading Mark is pointing upwards. When altering course the Heading Mark will turn and the image has to be reset.

CPA Closest point of approach. The minimum distance between two ships in a meeting situation. This distance can be determined in advance with a radar plot.

CRT (Cathode Ray Tube) The screen on older radar sets.

Cursor A convenient means of measuring bearing and range and handling a lot of other functions on the radar screen of a modern radar

Discrimination Range discrimination and bearing discrimination is the radar's ability to separate different contacts from each other.

Duct Abnormal refraction.

EBL Electronic bearing line.

Echo The reflected energy returning from a target. In some books the term Echo is used instead of contact.

Echo Stretch A function that makes contacts bigger.

Expansion See Echo Stretch

False contacts Apparent contacts without real targets. They are usually caused by reflected pulses.

Floating EBL A special EBL with a starting point that can be moved on the screen.

Floating VRM A VRM that can be moved on the screen.

FTC (Fast Time Constant) Another name for Anti-clutter rain.

Gain A function which amplifies the incoming echoes.

GPS A positioning device which can be interfaced to the radar set.

Guard zone or circle An area on the radar screen determined by the operator. When contacts appear in the Guard area, the radar will sound an alarm.

Head-up A presentation mode with your vessel in the centre of the image and the Heading Mark pointing upwards. Fixed targets move down the screen and moving targets are presented with a relative motion.

Heading The direction of the vessel in relation to true north.

Heading Mark or **Heading Line** A line on the radar screen, starting in the centre of the image and pointing in the boat's direction.

Indirect Contacts See False contacts.

Interface To connect other electronic devices (such as a compass or GPS) to the radar.

Interference Annoying contacts caused by another radar sending on the same or nearly the same frequency.

Interference rejection A means to reduce the effect of interference.

LCD (Liquid Crystal Display) The usual type of display on modern radars.

North-up A stabilized presentation mode in which north is up on the screen and the Heading Mark is pointing in the direction of the course. When altering course, only the Heading Mark turns.

Magnetron The part in the transmitter that actually produces the microwave pulses.

Off centre, Offset A radar display option that allows the centre of the image to be moved. It gives a longer Range forward without losing clarity close by. **Open array** A radar antenna that is not covered by a radome.

Overlay This is when the radar image is superimposed over an electronic chart.

Parallel index Allows the navigator to monitor the vessel's progress.

Plot To mark systematically the position of contacts of other vessels on the screen or on a plotting sheet and to draw conclusions from it.

PPI (Plan Position Indicator) An old expression for the radar screen.

Pulse The short burst of energy, transmitted by a pulse-emitting radar. Different ranges demand different pulse lengths.

Racon An active radar transponder located on, for example, a buoy or a lighthouse. It transmits a signal when hit by a radar pulse.

Radar lobe A radar beam.

Radar horizon The greatest distance at which the radar pulses can reach the sea level. To get a contact from a target behind the radar horizon, the target has to be sufficiently high.

Radar shadowing Occurs because the radar does not register objects behind and lower than the foreground.

Rain Clutter Disturbing contacts from rain, which can hide more useful contacts.

Rain Clutter control A means to reduce the annoying Rain Clutter.

Radome A cover that protects the antenna.

Range The distance from the centre of the radar image to its outer edge.

Range rings Fixed, concentric rings used for measuring distance.

Raster scan A type of radar screen, similar to a TV screen.

Refraction Depending on weather the radar beams bend more or less, increasing or decreasing the distance to the radar horizon.

Relative motion The motion made by contacts on the screen when using Head-up, North-up or Course-up mode. Fixed objects move parallel to Heading Mark and contacts from moving targets have a motion that is a combination of the own vessel's and the other vessel's movement.

Risk of collision According to the Colregs, risk exists when the bearing to the other vessel is not changing substantially.

Rule 19 Applies in restricted visibility to vessels not in sight of each other.

SART (Search and Rescue Transponder) A rescue aid for use in liferafts. When activated, the SART signal shows up on the radar screens of vessels in the vicinity as 12 dots.

S-band radar Has a 10cm wavelength, and is used on big ships.

Scanner Another word for antenna.

Sea Clutter Annoying contacts from waves close to the vessel, more from the windward side than the leeward.

Side Lobe Contacts Unwanted contacts caused by the antenna leaking energy outside the main radar beam.

SOG Speed over ground.

Stabilized The image is said to be stabilized when a heading sensor maintains the locations of contacts on the screen in specific orientation. North-up and Course-up are stabilized modes.

Standby The radar is not transmitting, but is ready to do so.

STC (Sensitivity Time Control) Another name for Anti-clutter Sea.

Sub-refraction Reduces the distance to the radar horizon.

Super-refraction Increases the distance to the radar horizon.

Target Whatever is reflecting the radar pulse (targets are sometimes referred to as contacts).

TCPA The time until the closest point of approach (CPA).

Trail The history of a contact's movement on the screen.

True motion A stabilized presentation mode in which the vessel is moving through the image with its own speed and heading. True motion needs to be interfaced to a position sensor (GPS) or a log and a compass.

Tune The adjustment of the radar's receiver to the frequency of its own transmitter. Can be manual or automatic.

Unstabilized The mode of a traditional Head-up mode without heading sensor.

Wake See Trail.

VRM (Variable Range Marker) An expanding electronic circle on the display used for measuring distances on the screen.

X-band Radar works on a 3cm wavelength and is usually found in all small craft radars.

Zoom function A means to enlarge a specific area and display that area in another part of the screen.

Published by Adlard Coles Nautical
an imprint of A & C Black Publishers Ltd
36 Soho Square, London W1D 3QY
www.adlardcoles.com

Copyright © Börje Wallin

First edition published 2010

ISBN 978-1-4081-1375-2

A CIP catalogue record for this book is available from the British Library.

This book is produced using paper that is made from wood grown in managed, sustainable forests. It is natural, renewable and recyclable. The logging and manufacturing processes conform to the environmental regulations of the country of origin.

Typeset in 10pt Sabon

Printed and bound in Singapore by Star Standard